# RIVER'S WAY

1  *Oregon badge on emperor's surcoat showing the primal dragon, symbol of the creative element behind change (Royal Ontario Museum)*

By the same author

*Dreambody*
*Working with the Dreaming Body*

**Arnold Mindell**

# RIVER'S WAY

The process science of the dreambody

Information and channels in dream and bodywork,
psychology and physics, Taoism and alchemy

**Routledge & Kegan Paul**
London and New York

To Marie Louise von Franz

First published in 1985
by Routledge & Kegan Paul Ltd

11 New Fetter Lane, London EC4P 4EE
England

Published in the USA by
Routledge & Kegan Paul Inc.
in association with Methuen Inc.
29 West 35th St., New York, NY 10001, USA

Set in Linotype Palatino 10/12 pt
by Columns of Reading
and printed in Great Britain
by Thetford Press Limited
Thetford, Norfolk

Library of Congress Cataloging in Publication Data

Mindell, Arnold, 1940-

River's way.
Bibliography: p.
Includes index.
1. Change (Psychology)   2. Change   3. Dreams.
4. Psychotherapy.    5. Human information processing.
I. Title.
BF637.C4M56    1985    150,19'54    85-2278

British Library CIP data also available

ISBN 0-7102-0631-3 (pbk.)

# CONTENTS

# ACKNOWLEDGMENTS

There are many real and dream people who helped me to develop process science. Jung's voice for example stirred me towards increasing empiricism. He became a model for me of someone who recognized and respected limitations and then transcended their restrictiveness. His attitude towards dreamwork, namely of returning to the dream's night-time journey for orientation and guidance is reflected in the present work in the concept of following the many-channeled process. He introduced me to alchemy and Taoism and together with his collaborator, M.L. von Franz, led me to the historical foundations behind process work.

Fritz Perls encouraged me through his games with the hot seat to extravert the unconscious and try to get away with it. Behaviorists such as Grinder and Bandler challenged me to discover the unconscious in their behaviorist's reality. Modern physicists like Richard Feynman indirectly helped me to understand that non-causal phenomena such as synchronicity require new concepts such as time reversal and anti-matter and that physics needs the psychology of the observer. Physicists such as Bohm and Finkelstein amazed me by implying that science was also searching for process theory. Einstein instigated my field theories and relativization of channels. Swami Muktananda made me realize that my fascination for process was equivalent to his worship of Shakti. I was just as surprised to find a verification and foundation for the idea of process work in Muktananda's Siddha Yoga as I was in finding this foundation in alchemy, Taoism and the mythology of time. Furthermore, Muktananda opened my eyes to the mythical emptiness of western body work.

Process science rests upon Jung's teleological attitude towards the collective unconscious, gestalt-oriented process work, Buddhist meditation, electronic communication theory and the phenomenological attitude of theoretical physics. Without these religions, psychologies and physical sciences, I could not have done my work. The present work has also grown out of the research presented in my *Dreambody* and *Working With the Dreaming Body* on the connections between dreams and body phenomena.

I am especially grateful to certain special seminar participants and co-workers in the Zürich, Switzerland, and Denver, Colorado, areas who joined me during the experimental phases of this work. Some of these people were Barbara Croci, Joe Goodbread, Nora Mindell, Max and Debbie Shüpbach, Carl Mindell, Roy Freeman, Pearl Mindell, Marilyn Raff, Glen and Jean Carlson, Amy Kaplan, Jean Claude and Giesela Audergon, Dawn Menken, Elke Müller, Julie Diamond, Urs Buttikoffer, and Victoria Herman. Special thanks to Jan Dworkin for her suggestions and critical reading of this work and to M.L. von Franz for her tireless interest in discussing the connection between psychological theory and empirical reality.

# Part I
# PROCESS AND CHANNELS

# Chapter I
# INTRODUCTION

This text attempts to assemble the empirical events appearing in dream, body, relationship and synchronicity phenomena within one theoretical framework and related technique. The thesis of this book is that accurate observation of the dreaming process interweaving the background of these phenomena together with the ability to sensitively follow these observations allows processes to unfold in the richest and most useful manner as judged by the observer. *River's Way* suggests that information process concepts may be used as a basis for dealing with a wide spectrum of events now separately considered by the various forms and schools of medicine, physics and psychology.

In the first part of the book, basic information channels of human processes are discussed and related to recent developments in physics. Part II traces the roots of process ideas in mythology, alchemy and Taoism. The resulting development of observational, theoretical and practical techniques, called process-oriented psychology, should be considered as one possible suggestion for approaching psycho-physical events without changing professionals, schools of thought or nations.

*An example*
Consider a typical wide-spectrum human problem. Think of a woman who came to see me because she was terrified about dying from a breast tumor. The content of her conversation, the verbs she used and her body gestures

3

indicated that her process was flowing at the moment through her body. 'I feel this lump in my breast and am scared of the pain,' she said. But instead of feeling or experiencing this pain further, she decided to quickly pull up her blouse so that I could examine her tumor. When I hesitated and asked her why she was so quick to show me her breast she told me that doctors always asked her to take off her clothes. I asked, 'Why do you believe other people's ideas more than your own feelings about yourself?'

She immediately launched into a painful story about how she had always overvalued others' opinions about herself, and how she had tried a lot to gain the approval of men because she did not believe in herself. Spontaneously she told me a dream about a pair of lovers who had been beaten up, in part because they did not ask the world around them for approval. One of these dream lovers was apparently wounded in the chest. We then talked about the conflict between her own love feelings for herself and the disapproval of the world around her. We spoke about the possible connection between the dream and her tumor and then she put her hand on her chest to feel her conflict and wounding.

The next day her husband appeared for a session and attacked me for wanting to see her breast. He wanted to know if I wanted to sleep with her. In the midst of this session, his wife walked in and we continued the conversation as a threesome. After assuring him that I was not interested in his wife as a sexual partner, we worked on his affects and it turned out that he was interested in flirting with women but that his (inner) mother was angry at him for having sexual fantasies. The work focused upon him. As he worked she was moved to express many locked-up feelings about him. Something like a family-oriented psychotherapy evolved. They left very happily.

Now, let us go back to her once again, and examine her process. She first focused upon a somatic channel, her body problem. Then her relationship with me became an issue for both of us. She then moved into a visual channel and told me a dream and finally returned to her body at the end of the first session. In the next session, her husband appeared, and her problems reappeared, this time reversed and mirrored in him. Finally their communication became the focus of our work.

This woman's process moved through various channels in a typical wide spectrum of behavior. She would have lost something by sending her body to a surgeon (by the way, her tumor, probably a cyst, disappeared by itself several weeks after the session) one part of her to a family therapist, another part to a dream analyst and another part still to a massage salon. She had one process with many interconnected aspects.

I want to point out here that the various aspects of personal life which psychology has referred to until now as dreams, body life, relationship conflicts and illness, can be re-evaluated in terms of sensory-oriented channels such as proprioception, kinesthesis, visualization, audition and compositions of these channels. Instead of talking about terms such as psychotherapy, body work, dream work, analysis, family therapy, we can now speak of process work.

I would expect any well-trained psychologist to be able to deal with a multitude of situations. I would also expect him to let things transform as they want to and not try to organize them himself. To do this he will have to discover the pattern behind the process of a given individual situation and base his work upon the nature of this pattern and its flow. The process worker no longer needs preprogrammed psychotherapeutic strategies or other routine methods of dealing with people. As a process scientist he can follow any given individual or family situation by using observational accuracy to discover the nature of processes. He uses a wide-spectrum analysis which applies to situations in which he is alone, with one or more people or events. He listens to the verbs people use, watches their body motions, notices his own reactions, discovers those he tends to neglect and determines experiences and follows processes according to their distance from individual or collective awareness, the channels which they manifest and their time patterns. Thus he not only lets the river flow but appreciates its exact nature. Experience with a wide range of people both normal and 'psychotic', healthy and dying, children and adults, individuals and families indicates that empirically following individual and group processes can be learned and substituted for 'pre-packaged' therapeutic programs.

Sound like Taoism? Process work is modernized Taoism in the sense that the process worker tries to appreciate the flow of the river and to help clients adjust to this flow. In fact, as I was developing process science, I felt a bit Chinese myself. I understood Lao Tsu who wrote in Chapter 21 of this three thousand year old *Tao Te Ching*, that the greatest virtue is to follow the Tao even though it seems dark, dim and elusive. For within the Tao, there is reality and reason. Process is deep and essential in its orientation. Like Lao Tsu, the process worker is also in the dark about the ultimate origin of change, though unlike the great old master, he has modernized Taoism so that it can be applied to life in an exact and empirical way.

No wonder I dreamed the other night of Lao Tsu, who was staying up late working behind a printing press. The idea of the Tao is very old, and appears again and again wherever an effort is made to unify the sciences upon the basis of energy concepts and empirical observations.

## UNIFYING MODERN PSYCHOLOGY

Already, many years ago the need for unifying psychology was felt and the hope for reconciliation expressed. Over thirty years ago Jung said the following.:

> I would remind you of the Liebault-Bernheim-Kreich method of suggestive therapy, reeducation de la Volonté; Babins Kils 'persuasion'; Dubois' 'traditional psychic orthopedics,'; Freud's psychoanalysis, with its emphasis on sexuality and the unconscious; Adler's educational method, with its emphasis on power drives and conscious fictions; . . . Each of them rests on special psychological assumptions and produces special psychological results, comparison between whom is difficult and often well-nigh impossible. Consequently it was quite natural that the champions of any one point of view should, in order to simplify matters, treat the opinions of the others as erroneous. Objective appraisal of the facts shows, however, that each of these methods and

theories is justified up to a point, since each can boast not only of certain successes but of psychological data that largely prove its particular assumption. Thus we are faced in psychotherapy with a situation comparable with that in modern physics where, for instance, there are two contradictory theories of light. And just as physics does not find this contradiction unbridgeable, so the existence of many possible standpoints in psychology should not give grounds for assuming that the contradictions are irreconcilable and the various views merely subjective and therefore incommensurable.[1]

Jung's early intuitions about the connections between psychology and physics and his amazing tolerance towards apparently contradictory psychotherapies are shared by many therapists today. It seems clear to me that as we approach the end of the twentieth century, the modern client's growing need to experience and understand the most extreme aspects of the personality is slowly being followed by the therapist's attempt to develop integrative process and energy theories in psychology. I expect this attempt to continue for a long time, for it is sorely needed.

Energy and process ideas in physics and psychology have been employed sporadically since the late 1960s to bridge the gaps in psychology created by nationality, sex and typology. We are not meditators or analyzers, with or without bodies, masculine or feminine, thinkers or feelers, dead or alive, but in varying degrees and at different times some impossible mixture of all these things. Stressing one aspect of the personality such as the development of the 'body' or the 'feminine' is obviously important at a given time in life. But stressing one aspect of the personality over long periods of time impoverishes another aspect and separates the individual as well as psychology into parts. This book should be understood as an effort at bridging unnecessary divisions in psychotherapy, medicine and physics.

This is also a good point to mention that after much reflection, I have chosen to use the unfortunate term 'he' in the sentences where I speak generally. I have done this because a simpler, neutral he/she term does not yet exist.

This is a sign, to me at least, that process concepts have not yet entered into our language. Future writers will certainly improve such linguistic defects.

The need to develop process concepts, however, is not based upon merely academic or theoretical considerations. Process is an empirical reality. Work with clients shows clearly that specific psychotherapies and medical rituals are definitely commensurable. In fact they are spontaneous creations which arise by amplifying events in given channels of the 'therapist-client' interaction even when the two are unfamiliar with these therapies. For example, if the process worker (kinesthetically) amplifies a client's repeated tendency to stretch, yawn and groan, specific postures from ancient yoga and modern bioenergetics appear as part of a fluid flow of events.[2] If he works verbally with the repressed sexual life of a theologian he will soon find proprioceptive experience which encourages the client to let himself enjoy pleasure along the lines of Wilhelm Reich.[3] If he works with the slow kinesthetic activity of a paralyzed person, processes mirroring the work of Feldenkrais appear.[4] A shy woman who visualizes violent encounters may have a process which switches from fantasy to violent interaction which one can find in restructuring processes used by Ida Rolf.[5] A client who uses her fingers to explain a migraine is indicating the specific proprioceptive process typical of acupuncture.[6]

If the process worker amplifies the tendency of a dreamer to speak to a particular dream figure during a dream report, then he develops a type of Black Elk dream ritual,[7] psychodrama[8] or active imagination.[9] A process worker observing the breathing of a homosexual man trying to cope with sexual excitement may rediscover Taoist Alchemy's transformation of energies.[10] A young person burdened by social conventions and parental complexes who tends to 'lose his mind in order to come to his senses' unravels the gestalt psychology of Fritz Perls.[11] A reflective woman in need of exact information about her behavior and conflict with her husband can create transactional analysis.[12]

A dying person's proprioceptive channel may use a binary system of communication with pain typical of the neurolinguistic programmer's 'reframing' method.[13] If you study the way parents talk about their kids you can develop behavioral psychology with its causal orientation and stimulus-response theory.[14] Let your clients bring their family members to their sessions, study their relationship channels and you create family therapy.[15] Trace a man's interest in connecting his dreams with his conscious problems, study the legends and myths typical of his dreams and you begin to rediscover Jungian psychology.[16] Follow parapsychology and you enter theoretical physics.[17] Move with your client, encourage his non-verbal expressions and you begin to develop dance therapy.

Thus it is useful but insufficient in process work to know the hundreds of therapy rituals because each of them appears spontaneously when the client's signals and therapy situation are followed. Process work cannot be described in terms of events because its structure and evolution are created from changing signals, channels and amplifications. Process work begins with whatever presents itself, the client's questions, problems in relationship, medical symptoms, stories of the day before, dream experiences or even the therapist's problems, and uses verbal processes, language content, body signals and environmental situations to determine the nature and evolution of the client-therapist interaction. Process work, accurately carried out, often reveals the meaning of dreams before they have been reported because the work deals with the living unconscious, that is dreaming phenomena occurring at the edge of the client's awareness.

Process work or any other psychotherapy succeeds only when the therapist is able to function in the client's momentary channel, and not because of the general validity of the therapist's education about that channel.

The therapist's successful feelings are not enough. Process science checks on the validity of its work by assessing the verbal feedback, the client's body responses and dreams.

As we approach the end of the twentieth century, psychology is blossoming in a dramatic fashion. Increasing understanding of the personality together with powerful therapeutic techniques are making it necessary for therapists trained in one specialty to increase their ability in other forms of work. It seems almost essential that a process orientation develops in psychology to unify research and practice. However, as energy theories become increasingly popular throughout the world of psychology, clarity and theoretical fundamentalness should also increase to prevent psychology from regressing backwards to shamanism.

The necessity for developing an accurate process work, though apparently obvious, will be a continuous challenge for therapists because it is not simple to have a beginner's mind and create or adjust the work to the flow of information occurring between client and therapist. Years of experience in training students and therapists from various schools of psychology have convinced me in the advantages and disadvantages of educational systems favoring one particular channel.

For example, 'process oriented' dance therapists tend to ignore relationship issues which arise with their clients, and are usually not strong in supporting a client's intellectual needs. Massage therapists are powerful in relating to the proprioceptive channels of their clients but are usually not trained to encourage verbal feedback or spontaneously arising movement processes. Dream-centred therapies often neglect dance and body experiences. Classical gestalt therapists will not support research; behaviorists do not listen to fantasies.

Thus specific belief systems, typological variations and previous education allow the therapist to become aware of only some of his client's signals. Knowing this limitation should help us remain humble and also to retain a beginner's mind when working with signals and channels which are different from the ones we may have studied. It is useful to re-member that great advances in science have always occurred whenever new channels were added to accepted and predeter-mined categories in the face of empirical evidence which did not fit these categories. Today, there's so much of this evidence clustering around dying, physical illness, mental disturbances, parapsychology and relationship issues that we should feel free to doubt what we now know and to open up to more comprehensive frameworks of reference.

# Chapter 2
# ELEMENTS OF PROCESS SCIENCE

In this chapter I wish to give the reader a concise and general view of process theory.

PROCESS
I use the word process to refer to changes in perception, to the variation of signals experienced by an observer. The observer's personality determines which signals he picks up, which he is aware of and which he identifies himself with and therefore which he reacts to. The interaction between the observer and signals is discussed in greater detail in chapter 5.

A useful and naturally incomplete analogy in thinking about the term process is to compare it to a train and its stations. Process refers to the travels of this train. Sometimes observations begin with signals coming from Sick City, or Troublesville, sometimes from Happiness Town, sometimes from Death's corner. The observer gets on the train at these and other places and rides the train to wherever it takes him. Process is like a special train whose destination can not always be predicted. The observer follows the signals in his real life or in a fantasy trip as they reveal life to him.

PROCESSES AND STATES
The very idea of process contrasts with the idea of a fixed state, which is a static picture, an unchanging description of a situation which has been broken up into parts. Saying that the train process is in the state called Headache City or

Relationship Junction tells us that the process is in a certain state with a certain name. States are useful descriptions of processes. Claiming that a process is in Headache City, however, only tells us one of its states. If we get on the train where it is, in Headache City, it will go anywhere, anyplace its locomotive driver will take it.

Personal temperament of the researcher or client determines whether one focuses upon states, processes or both. Its seems essential to develop a process-oriented psychology which includes both. In process work, static unchanging conditions are defined as specific processes so that theory and practice closely follow living change and evolution. State-oriented psychology reduces living material to fixed patterns and programs. Thus, pressing a client's language into 'here and now' vocabulary, deciding to be helpful before meeting a client, wanting to heal without reference to the symptoms, or deciding relationships should be harmonious, then you are a state-oriented therapist who does not work with the changing processes which your patients may really have.

Of course, state-oriented psychology can be very valuable because its fixed routines give people the feeling of safety and predictability. Everyone needs at one time or another this stability. Thus your process may be, for a short time or even over a long period of time, working within a very exact and routine framework. State work becomes inadequate and inapplicable however, when stationarity gives way to flow and when given routines begin to inhibit experience.

**PRIMARY AND SECONDARY PROCESSES**
Processes can be static or moving. They can also be described as being closer or further from awareness. If I look at a train for example, I can see that it is, as a whole, running smoothly. Let us say that it has six cars and that at first sight all are moving nicely together. However at closer inspection we see that one of the cars has smoke coming out of one of its windows. We tend to ignore the smoke and say that the train is fine unless the smoke gets so heavy that it disturbs the whole train. Steady forward movement of the

train is its primary process; its smoking caboose is its secondary process. People identify themselves with their intentions or primary processes. Secondary processes are experienced as being foreign and distant. For example, you may be a very sweet and decent person, as a whole. You identify yourself with your sweetness and decency. But every now and then you become a monster. This monster is something which happens to you. You feel it is not characteristic of you. As far as you are concerned, it just pops out of you every now and then. Being a monster is your secondary process. Being sweet is the primary one.

CONSCIOUS AND UNCONSCIOUS

It has been practical until now to use the terms conscious and unconscious for primary and secondary processes. Process science has to redefine these earlier terms because they are not always useful empirically in their present form. For example, in psychotic states, near death phenomena and deep body experiences the terms 'conscious and unconscious' become meaningless. So let us say that from now on consciousness refers only to those processes of which you are completely aware. When you are conscious, you notice the signals you are receiving, you are not simply receiving them but are aware of your awareness. In other words, you not only feel or see something, you are aware of the fact that you are feeling or seeing this something.

Unconsciousness refers to all other types of signal processes. Thus if I am absolutely aware of how I experience and know I am sweet and decent, then I am conscious of this process. Otherwise sweetness and decency cannot be controlled, I may even say that I know that I am sweet and decent, and yet be unconscious of how sweetness processes really overtake me. Then they are primary processes, they happen outside my control and are unconscious.

Nevertheless getting in touch with sweetness is going to be easier for me than getting in touch with my monster for it is secondary, it is much further away from my awareness. I do not identify myself with the monster. Hence every secondary process presents us with a sort of identity crisis.

However, the more aware and conscious we are the more we realize that we are a combination of many processes which may be occurring simultaneously or one after the other.

## CHANNELS

Thus processes can be identified in terms of their being static or moving and also in terms of their being close to or far from our self identity. Another very typical and powerful way of differentiating processes is in terms of the signals in which they appear to us. For example, the ancient Chinese, whose culture was based upon the Tao or process of change, said that the Tao could manifest itself in essentially three channels, Heaven, Earth and Man. Modern psychologists have spoken about the personality in terms of mind, matter, psyche and more recently, relationships. Buddhist meditators speak in terms of senses which perceive specific signals, in terms of smelling, tasting, touching, hearing and seeing.

There is no one way of differentiating processes in terms of channels. It is important to realize that given channels reflect specific individuals and/or cultures. In this book, several types of channel systems will be discussed. The process scientist does not fasten himself to one particular channel system but is, theoretically, able to observe himself and a given situation and discover what channels his client or family situation is operating with. Thus he becomes fluid in his observational system and does not try to make a situation fit his categories of mind or body, especially when phenomena themselves may relativize his dimensionalizations. Thus for example, psychosomatic problems and parapsychological events make channels such as mind and body, matter and psyche look mystical because they are inappropriate tags put on events which come with other tags already on them.

The most common sensory channels appearing in one-to-one work with clients appear to be visualization, audition, body feeling or proprioception and body movement or kinesthesis. Other channels such as relationships are mixtures of these basic ones. In this book we shall focus mainly upon the basic channels and the amazing ability of processes to switch almost unpredictably from one channel to another. In a future work, I focus on the channels of couples, families and groups.

## BASIC CHANNELS

Signals may be differentiated according to the perception sense which picks them up. Signals and processes are therefore channeled by our senses. We can therefore visualize, hear, we can feel with our bodies, we can sense movement, we can smell, taste and use combinations of these senses to apprehend signals and processes.

Channels are like the tracks upon which the process train moves, the potential directions of the river. We get on our train upon a certain track. If it leaves from Track 1, then our process may be manifesting itself through the channel of visualization. Track 2 is frequently hearing. Track 3 is body feeling, or proprioception and Track 4 for Americans and Europeans is usually kinesthesis, that is the sense of movement. Tracks 5 and 6 are generally compositions of the first four tracks. Smell and taste do not often play a significant role in the majority of processes and hence will not be discussed in detail in this work.

In any case your process may begin by getting on your train on Track 2, at Headache's Corner. At some point outside of town the train probably switches to Track 3 before it arrives in Peaceville. In other words, you began to follow your process when you got a headache. Internal dialogue may have been in the foreground of your awareness before you began to feel the pounding of your head and before your process began to give you some peace.

## VISUALIZATION

Now let us look at the main channels which come up most frequently in one to one process work and discuss them in some detail. We shall be dealing with the basic channels, visualization, audition, proprioception and kinesthesis, the detailed or 'fine structure' of these channels and their combinations.

The visual channel is usually best developed and most familiar to us. We use our sight more than our taste or hearing. Vision gives us the ability to know things at great distance, it allows us to gain emotional distance from phenomena, it organizes what we normally call insight. The modern founders of psychology began their studies with what we are now calling the visual channel. Freud felt that the royal road to the unconscious was dreams. Jung pioneered in the study of images and the use of active imagination, a purposeful confrontation with these images which also includes audition that is listening to these images. Perls centered his work around dreams as well.

The process worker amplifies signals according to their channel and nature. Thus if a dream report stresses the color of an image, its intensity, content or story he will work with intensification of the color, intensity, amplifying its content with mythological images or encouraging the dreamer to tell more about the drama in the dream thereby gaining more courage to let the story unfold. He may also play a part of the dream and ask the dreamer to view the drama while he, the process worker, acts it out. In other words, the dream work depends very much upon how the dreamer tells the dream and what methods he uses while telling it.

The existence of process in the visual channel can be determined by the fact that the client's eyes or head move upward, by the client's use of sentences such as 'do you see', 'I need insight', or 'I am seen' or 'they look at me', or by the predominance of breathing movements located in the upper chest.

AUDITION

When the eyes move to the right or left, when sentences and statements such as 'listen to me, hear me, speak more loudly please, I can not hear you, that sounds nice, etc.' appear, or when body posture 'freezes' without the head going down, processes in the auditory channel are occurring.

Amplification of these processes occurs by increasing focus upon the tone in which sounds are being emitted, becoming aware of their tempo and rhythm, their musical nature, their verbal content, by determining the nature of internal dialogues, according to whether it is connnected to human or inanimate sources, etc.

## PROPRIOCEPTION

Visual and auditory processes have been discussed in the literature more than proprioceptive and kinesthetic signals. The next chapter will therefore concentrate upon proprioception and kinesthesis.

Proprioception is usually indicted by predominance of stomach breathing, eyelid flutters (with closed eyes) or when the signaler speaks of feeling, pressure, depression, pain, joy, being turned off or on. This channel usually lies in the foreground of awareness when there are long periods of no talking coupled with eyes looking downwards; when the head drops, when people speak of falling or when hands touch painful areas. Amplification in the proprioceptive channel occurs according to the nature of the signal. The individual in a proprioceptive channel can intensify focus upon an inner feeling such as a stomach ache, sleeping foot or sexual excitement by not moving. Or the therapist can amplify pressures and pains by pushing, rolling, vibrating or lifting a body area, and observing how proprioception deepens and flows into other channels such as movement.

## KINESTHESIS

Process work deals with kinesthetic activity by perceiving the nature of the movement or lack of movement in the face hands, legs and torso. Body energy often evolves from one motion into a posture, into other movements and dance or into other channels. Amplification may accur through mirroring movement, encouraging it verbally, actually touching and propelling the dancer, not talking or looking at him, or even by temporarily interrupting his movement.

## THE FINE STRUCTURE OF THE BASIC CHANNELS

The signals which appear in the form of seeing, hearing proprioceping and the sense of movement differentiate themselves in terms of what we may call, the 'fine structure of channels.' [I am thankful to Dr Joe Goodbread of Zurich for recommending this term to me.] People spontaneously tell you that they see things 'inside,' hear 'real' or 'outer' voices, experience other people 'feeling for them' or find that they can mix channels and see with their bodies for example. We can generalize these experiences by referring to signals as being introverted, extraverted, referred or mixed. Let me explain these terms in greater detail.

### INTROVERTED SIGNALS
The introverted seer looks up into the air, gazes off into the distance or closes his eyes and says, while holding his breath, that he is visualizing some internal scene not necessarily seen by others. A person gifted in this mode of perception considers himself a fantasiful person, an artist or even photographer. He claims to see through things, may be a medium or mystic.

Introverted hearing picks up internal dialogue, particular voices from the past, though music and strange internal sounds often fill this channel as well. The introverted proprioceptor is highly aware of his internal body experiences and orients himself according to these. He knows when he is uncomfortable and adjusts himself accordingly. Introverted kinesthesis picks up dream-like movements and is aware of the tendency to move even before a limb has begun to tighten up or relax. Introverted kinesthesis refers to the experience of moving without actually having done anything with the body and is usually referred to as 'out of the body experience.'

### EXTRAVERTED SIGNALS
Extraverted signals refer to information which is usually part of what the people around one call reality. The extraverted seer for example notices the colors and shapes of other people's clothes, he notices how people look when they are happy and sad. He can develop this function to pick up double signals in people's movement, and may use his internal visualizing capacity to even imagine what sort of

dream is being portrayed by movement which is not directly explained by the other person.

The extraverted hearing channel focuses upon the content of what others say, and is aware of the sounds of the natural environment. Thus function may be developed to also pick up the tempo and tonality of sound as well. Extraverted proprioception picks up the body experience of others through the medium of one's own touch. The masseur has usually developed the proprioceptive ability of his hands or elbows. Extraverted proprioception and kinesthesis usually are necessary for all non-verbal contact and sexual experience. Extraverted kinesthesis gives you a sense and ability to move in a congruent and graceful manner. Someone with little extraverted kinesthesis cannot throw a ball or may appear very awkward while walking and running. This person may not be able to follow someone else while dancing. This function is usually developed in early childhood, and later left untouched by conscious focus.

### COMPOSITE SIGNALS

Physiology refers to the most common mixed signals as synaesthesia. Thus people on LSD sometimes hear with the bones in their legs, sometimes people say that they can see through their shoulders or the back of the head. Others claim to be able to dance with their eyes, visualize while simultaneously dancing and hearing internal music. The process worker may deal with these mixed phenomena by encouraging them to occur by using the same language with which they are described. In this way he deals with psychosomatic and parapsychological phenomena without having to call these phenomena by such complicated names.

Thus besides the fundamental channels called seeing, hearing, feeling, moving and their fine structures, there are other important channels which are compositions of these fundamental sensory perceptions. The special natures of these compositions may vary from person to person, yet the general quality of these compositions is that they can not be broken down into more fundamental components without disturbing the overall perception.

For example, you may say that you are highly aware of other people and that this awareness is based upon love without being able to say how you love in terms of seeing, hearing, moving, etc. Your loving awareness of people, or your ability to sense and relate to the natural environment are composite channel experiences, that is you can not break down your sense of awareness into more fundamental sensory perceptions without destroying your ability to perceive.

The layman's use of terms like 'awareness' and 'consciousness' frequently refer to composite channel experiences. Thus individual channels such as seeing, hearing and feeling may all be inextricably combined in such a way that they are insufficient to explain the overall composite perception.

Jung further differentiated these irreducible composite channel experiences in terms of the special abilities of consciousness he called, thinking, feeling, intuition and sensation.[1] Thus some people typically function with their thinking in perceiving others and the world around them, they tend to discover logical structures while other people feel the patterns as beautiful or awful in their environment. Intuitives sense the whole of something but cannot discover its parts while the sensation type apprehends the details, the objects and parts of a whole without being able to grasp the whole. The reader interested in the complete study of Jung's typology should refer to literature on this topic.[2] For the moment, let it suffice to mention only that all channels are a function of time and that at any given moment a new channel may be characteristic of the foreground of awareness.

### RELATIONSHIP

The composite channel which I have termed, 'relationship' is referred to in discussions where people talk about another person with whom they are familiar as if this person were the central object of awareness. 'My husband is my big problem,' 'My girlfriend adores me,' 'My boss is constantly on my mind,' are statements which refer to extraverted aspects of relationships. The process worker deals with the extraverted relationship channel on the grounds of its basic nature and works together, where ever and whenever possible, simultaneously, with the outer person who is the focus of attention, together with the person making these statements.

Awareness in the relationship channel can be increased by noticing the client's behavior in the midst of relating to his partner. Alternatively the partner may be considered to be a channel for the client, or both partner and client may be understood as being channels for the relationship as a whole.

Introverted relating appears in dreams where one feels badly or is dealing with a dream figure in an inappropriate manner. Introverted relationship is then a function of gestalt imaginations or active imagination where one imagines or plays with the dream person as if it were a real person. A real outer person can be either an introverted or extraverted situation or process depending upon the client's experience of this person as being an inner problem, outer one or both. Trying to get a client to introvert a figure or work with the outer real person is thus a matter of the moment.

### THE WORLD

When focus pays attention to the outer world, the universe, unfamiliar people, foreign objects and events, then we might speak of a world channel. Introverted relationship to the world occurs when people 'sense' outer events, communicate with others at a distance, or feel influenced by the universe without actually moving outside their bedroom. These people may also say that trees speak to them, that rocks and animals can be their friends and that the mother earth is their relative.

Extraverted relationship to the world is based upon actually working with outer events, objects and people, jobs and money problems, being able to fix machines, care for plants, and be interested in the ecology of the earth. Obviously, the world channel is not well developed by most Americans or Europeans who have little conscious experience, either internally or externally of the world around them, its suffering and needs. Probably this is why many people feel the world is negative or chasing them.

## DIAGRAMS OF THE CHANNELS

It is fun and also instructive to place the main channels next to one another in the form of diagrams or lists. If we look at the first diagram on the next page we notice for example how channel theory makes it possible to differentiate and be more exact with earlier and vaguer terms such as mind, body and matter or world. The earlier term, 'mind' usually refers to seeing and hearing. The idea of body is usually a composition of feeling and moving. The universe is some composite channel which has meant the perception of family, nations and earth. Moreover, what has been referred to in general as consciousness and awareness either is a composition of this diagram or a specific aspect of it.

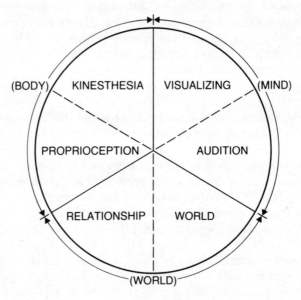

Diagram 1  *The channels*

## MAIN AND UNOCCUPIED CHANNELS

What happens to the channels not occupied by your awareness? They are often filled in by other people or objects or bodies! Often people experience others as

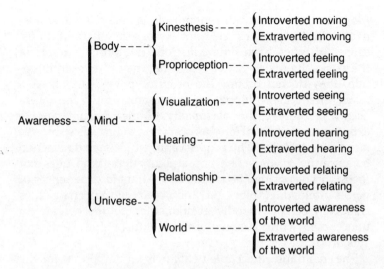

Diagram 2 *The fine structure of channels*

listening or seeing them. Other people are said to be able to feel for you, or they can move and do your activities when you feel paralyzed. If you make any of these statements then your hearing, seeing, body feeling and movement are 'unoccupied', that is you experience these channels as if they were in other people or objects. People who do not consciously use their eyes or ears usually experience these organs as if they were located in their friends or enemies. 'He sees me as I really am,' 'Only she can hear what I am truly saying,' 'My mother knows when I am hungry,' 'Thank God for my four-wheel-drive car, it can take me places I could never get by myself!' These statements indicate unoccupied sensory perception and can be worked with in practice by encouraging the creator of these sentences to imagine himself to be the person or object possessing his senses and to sense life through this person's or object's eyes, ears, etc.

At any given moment people identify themselves with particular channels, with their 'main' channels and tend to dissociate themselves from other channels. In the terms of

Jung, and in terms of the composite channels of consciousness, thinking types do not recognize their feelings, sensation types have little conscious intuition. In terms of the basic channels, visual types may have no proprioception, they do not occupy the proprioceptive channel. As a result phenomena happen in this channel as if they were occurring outside the personality of the visual type. He experiences body problems as occurring to him, as strokes of fate or as accidents. The proprioceptive type may be plagued by uncanny visions. The non-auditory type who does not focus on voices, may be plagued by paranoid experiences of voices following him. An occupied world channel is characterized by friendly relationships to the world, an unoccupied world channel is filled with fateful events and synchronicities.

The main and unoccupied channels are important for the process worker for if he can determine which channel is a primary one and which the unoccupied or secondary, then the main channel can be used to integrate irrational secondary processes. An unoccupied channel will bring the client the most powerful and uncontrolled experience. I will talk more about the main and unoccupied channels in the following chapters. Here, let me mention only that a visual type will need a language filled with visualizations in order to understand his body experiences, an auditory type will have to get the world to speak to him, a person suffering the wanton behavior of the world will need literal help in dealing with the transportation or job situation of a given city. A proprioceptor with little kinesthesia will suffer from broken limbs, an unoccupied relationship channel will be characterized by loving and hating processes originating outside the individual.

Total awareness and individuation or self-completion implies developing one's ability to pick up and deal with signals coming from all the channels. Processes often get blocked or stale-mated when people identify with only one or two of the above mentioned channels or with only their primary processes.

## AMPLIFICATION

The most powerful tool of the process worker is his ability to determine the evolving structure of processes, i.e. their channels, primary and secondary characteristics. His second most useful tool is his ability to work with signals in their own various channels, to amplify these signals and bring them closer to awareness. The exact nature of amplification depends on the individual client, therapist and the channel. There is no one set of techniques which will fit every situation. Part of the creativity of process work is learning the methods of amplification implied by the signals themselves.

For example, one way of amplifying a visual signal is by encouraging the individual to see more exactly what is happening. Introverted proprioception may be amplified by encouraging the client not to listen, look or feel anything outside himself. Kinesthesis may be amplified by encouraging movement without looking or listening. Working with the extraverted relationship channel may be encouraged by telling the client not to pay attention to himself, etc.

## EDGES AND CONGRUENCE

The point at which the client says, 'that I cannot do, or will not do', is the point where he has reached an edge. He may not be able to look at something, hear a certain voice or noise, make a certain movement, or feel a specific feeling like sex. He may not want to pay attention to a particular person in his environment, or deal with the world. The borders, the limits, the boundary of his personal ability tells you where his growing edge lies. Process work deals with the edge by staying near it, by switching channels and going around it, by letting it be, by jumping over it or by whatever means achieves positive feedback from the client.

The edge splits processes up into primary ones which the client identifies himself with and secondary ones which he feels are not directly associated with him. The edge contributes to making the individual congruent and incongruent or split. A visual person, for example, may not identify himself with his body feelings. Thus, when he gets a stomach ache, he refuses to realize his stomach is aching until it has become so severe that it incapacitates him. He says, his body is unimportant or that it cannot be felt and thus creates an edge which splits off his proprioception which then appears as a secondary phenomena which happens to him. He becomes incongruent insofar as he experiences two processes, one which he likes and is aware of, namely his visualization and another which he does not like, his stomach ache! Edges which continue for long periods of time develop into blocks and are associated with psychosomatic problems, apparently because information not consciously picked up is always rerouted through the body.

### SECONDARY PROCESS AND DOUBLE SIGNALS

Recall that the signals of which you are barely aware are secondary processes. While thinking, scratching can be a secondary process. While talking, the tone and tempo of your voice are likely to be secondary. These secondary processes become double signals when they are incongruent with primary processes. If you tell me you agree with me but simultaneously shake your head indicating 'no', then your head is giving me a double signal, a second message which is not congruent with the verbal yes. If you were to say 'yes' and nod accordingly then the secondary process would be congruent with the primary one and there would be no double signal but one central message instead.

Double signals are natural, normal human phenomena which occur as disturbances in communication with yourself and with someone else as well. They are a combined product of your spontaneous creativity, of the existence of channels which are not at your disposal, of conscious inhibitions and of your inability to admit paradox. Some double signals occur at the perimeter of your awareness, some are further away. An accurate process scientist discovers these double signals and amplifies them or their relationship to primary processes; he then works with the edges involved in the split.

**DREAMS AND PROCESSES**

One of the most exciting discoveries of process science is that the evolution which results from amplifying primary and secondary processes is always mirrored in dreams. Thus, process work is living dreamwork in the sense that when we work with the total process of an individual, we are working with his dreams. This discovery gives rise to the concept of the dreambody,[3] namely the idea that your secondary body processes such as illnesses and symptoms appear in dreams. Moreover, since secondary processes can appear in the form of double signals we can see the dreaming process in others as well and even guess their dreams.[4]

*An example*

Let us say for example that you are a visual type of person with little body awareness and that proprioception is a weak and unoccupied channel for you. Thus your feeling and movement may be projected upon or occupied by your car, for example. In any case, you are comfortable with visualization and organize your life accordingly.

One night you dream that your car is worn out and that a cop arrests you for driving a car which is not in order. The morning after the dream you awake feeling a bit ill, you have a stomach ache which you neglect, you have an edge against proprioception and think that it is less important than your plans for the day. You see yourself going shopping and thus you make the plans to go and ask the kids to join you. While you are talking to them you barely notice the double signals you are sending out, the signals related to your stomach ache. The kids see the pained expression on your face of which you are not aware and decide not to come. You get angry at them and have a fight and leave. On route to the store your unconscious proprioception, that is your stomach ache, amplifies itself until you get so sick that you are forced to go home. Symbolically speaking, a cop caught you with a worn out car and sent you home. If you do not occupy your proprioception, he will!

If you were a process worker and had no edge against

your body, you would have realized that you were worn out and you would have realized the meaning of your dream. You would have amplified your secondary processes, your stomach signals, perhaps put them together with your primary process, your visual plan to shop, and communicated more congruently with the kids and had a better day.

### SUMMARY OF CONCEPTS

The message of this tale is, be aware. These two words have been recommended by wise gurus since the beginning of time. Awareness could be a one-word book. Print it and send it around. The reason however why this wonderful recommendation has never quite succeeded is that people have edges against certain forms of awareness. Thus if you do not differentiate processes and signals into primary and secondary, and if you do not tell people about the channels and states they express they will 'forget' that such states exist!

Being a phenomenologist, a process scientist is a sort of a mystic and an empirical, rigorous scientist in one. He determines the existence of channels whose exact nature may never be completely understood and thus works with phenomena whose ultimate origins may even be unthinkable. Thus he discovers, without understanding why, that process flows like a river from one channel to another around edges, over objects, and ravines which only miracles could breach. He tries to follow the course of the river and adjust himself to its flow. He listens carefully to sentence structure, watches body signals, uses his hands to feel the dance of life and his imagination to explain his own responses.

When primary and secondary processes agree he speaks of congruence but when they are split off into double signals, body symptoms and communication problems he respects incongruity and satisfies himself with letting them be. In a world where the processes of nature such as sickness and health, death and life, love and hate remain outside his manipulation, he creates his own systems of belief, and leaves others to theirs. He lets nature show him the way and may even support unsolvable and painful situations without deluding himself with the naive superstition of the 'modern world' that personal and astronomical events are under his control.

# Chapter 3
# BODY CHANNELS

There are many processes which clients describe and experience which seem to have little or at least in the moment nothing to do with anyone else but themselves. Thus the world channels play a negligible role in these processes. Relationship channels and natural events are not essential parts of the work. In these situations we can talk about dreambody work by which we mean that the client's process remains in the visual, auditory, proprioceptive and kinesthetic channels. For study purposes then it is convenient to talk about these four channels together. In the following two chapters relationship and world channels are discussed.

When someone centers on a dream or body problem, then the process worker can assume that the relationship channel does not play a central role if there is no particular difficulty between process worker and client. When someone says that he wants to work on a dream then I make an attempt to notice just how the dreamer indicates that the dreamwork is to be done. I follow his primary process, that is his conscious problems and specific interests in a certain type of dreamwork, but I also pay strict attention to the method which the dreamer indicates while he is telling me the dream.

If he starts to speak with the dream figure while telling his dream then something like gestalt work or active imagination with that dream figure is likely to gain positive feedback on that part of the dream from the dreamer. If he stresses a certain word, uses a foreign term, stutters while saying a phrase or giggles while mentioning something, then I ask him to associate, fantasy about or amplify that particular work or phrase. If the dreamer is not able to do any of these things, or if he asks about the meaning of a certain situation or figure, then I might use Jung's idea of mythological amplification employing impersonal information to elucidate that specific part of the dream. If the dreamer unconsciously acts out certain parts of the dream, that is if he begins to show me what happened in the dream while telling it, then I might begin by asking him to recreate those postures and start from there.

Frequently the dreamer will put his hand on a particular part of his body, or move closer or further from me during his dream reportage. Repeating these gestures and movements is often revealing. Often the dreamer is not even primarily interested in his dreamwork. Then he tells the dream while double signalling. This means he sends out facial expressions or body gestures which give me incongruent information unrelated to his reportage. Then I begin with this incongruence in such cases.

The point I am trying to make is that I attempt to pick up the signals of the total process, and encourage partial verbal statements, incomplete body motions, and inconsistencies to unfold and reveal their entire messages. In this way dreamwork becomes ritualistic respect of the total personality's attempt to express and become itself.

Now I would like to give some specific examples of process work which focuses upon the flow of events happening in the moment. The reader who is looking for the more conventional type of case history should keep in mind that my focus here is not upon the client's entire life story or healing process. These aspects of psychology are important too and appear in process work when the client shows a spontaneous interest in telling his history or in asking me to help him recover from some illness or neurosis (of his definition). I neither encourage nor discourage such interest nor do I define my role in terms of healing or enlightenment.

As I have said before, I focus upon gaining positive verbal

and non-verbal feedback from the client and have discovered that this occurs most frequently when I let his
process and my momentary situation define the so called
'therapy situation'. Other forms of work seem to resist
nature, they exhaust the therapist and give the client the
experience of being misunderstood. Consider Ron.

### RON'S MUSIC

Ron is middle aged and suffers from depression. I have not
seen Ron for a long time. As I enter my office he is already
sitting on the floor and comments to me that I seem to be
really happy. He claims that he is depressed. When he
begins to tell me about his depression I notice that his voice
is very melodious, in a way which I have not heard before.
He prefers not to pick up my comment on his voice, and
insists that we work on one of his dreams.

He tells his dream like a story. 'Once there was a flute
player who loved his flute. My connection to the flute was
like the connection between matter and psyche.' I noticed
that he enjoyed talking about the dream and I asked him to
go on talking, to tell me a story about this dream. Though
he was depressed he picked up my recommendation and
told me about the flute player and his instrument in such
detail that he even began to act out certain motions of the
playing during his recitation. As he repeated these kinesthetic motions several times I recommended that he play
more, and before long he became the flute player and began
singing a lovely but sad tune. He finished, saying that he
felt really well, that his life was meaningful and that he was
not depressed because he got in touch with his deepest
feelings.

### PROCESS ANALYSIS

Ron's primary process was centered upon worrying about
his depression. His secondary process appeared in the
double signal of his voice (its melodiousness) and in the
figure of the flute player and the flute. By following his
interest in talking about his dreams, he began to do active
imagination with the dream figure by telling me a story

about this figure. Finally, by picking up on the musician's motions which Ron made while telling me the story it was possible for him to consciously connect to the musician in himself and with his own voice. This latter phenomena was gestalt-like in the sense of identifying with the motions of the dream figure. However, if I had asked him to do so in the beginning he could not have sung. Such a request would have skipped his interest in story telling. His process went through several channels according to an order which was characteristic of his particular situation, his and my psychology as well. In this process oriented dreambody work Ron's dream pictorialized the double signals in his voice. By following the channels of his process he was able to become more congruent, and then his depression lifted. By consciously occupying his own auditory channel, he had a strong experience, i.e. an awareness of his total self.

SAM'S INTROVERSION
Sam sat down and said that he was so tired that before he could speak he needed to close his eyes for a minute. Then I noticed that he moved his shoulders back and forth like people sometimes do when there is something frustrating them. I told him to amplify the motion until he said that something bothered him in (the pectoral muscles of) his chest. As he was moving his shoulders back and forth very gently I recommended that he do this with greater awareness. What happens, I said, when you move your shoulder a millimeter forward or a millimeter backwards? Immediately he said that moving forward was like being nice to people and moving backwards was moving into himself.

I let him make these motions spontaneously himself for a few moments until he suddenly made a discovery. He said, with excitement 'When I move backwards I can also be there for the other person, even though I am centered in myself.' This discovery was important to Sam who then told me how, as a therapist, he gets so tired by focusing upon others all the time. Before he left he told me a dream. In the dream a man was withdrawing from the sea into a house, and was throwing a tank of benzine back into the water. His two friends who stayed near the seaside saved the tank in the last minute.

In this work we see something which frequently happens in dreambody work. We can guess the dream from the body work. His dream tells us what we have already discovered. As a therapist, his introverted nature is fed up with extraverting and being open to others. Thus this part of him withdraws into his pectoral muscles and tends to make him introvert and meditate. From this comes a tank full of energy which is thrown into his work with others. That is why he gets so tired. The dream shows the possibility of saving this tank. In the work he learned to hold back his extraversion by introverting while extraverting, sitting back and then coming forward when he is ready.

In this work we see that Sam was interested primarily in talking to me but his proprioception stopped him. He had to sit back. His secondary process was withdrawing, his kinesthesis was unoccupied by his awareness. Working in a gentle way with movement, creating awareness through small motions, would be typical of the Feldenkrais method of body work. The important channels of this work were proprioceptive and kinesthesis. Through movement we investigated his 'housing' that is his withdrawing in order to be centered in his relationship to others.

In Sam's work we see that process work, follows the dreaming process. The dream itself can be used in Sam's work as a summary or a pictorialization of body processes. The dream, it seems, is a process trying to happen. Its symbols refer in part to body experiences which are trying to reach awareness.

### ESTHER'S DEVIL

As Esther and I began to chat, she put her hand on the back of her head and told me that she had a hard time sleeping the previous night because she had 'pressing' pains in her neck shooting down to her lower back. She repeated her hand motions several times. Thus I decided to repeat them consciously with her. I said, 'Let me put my hand on your back or neck and you tell me where it belongs.' In doing so I was using her body wisdom, her proprioception to direct my hand to do things her hand was trying to do. Once my hand was on her back she told me to put it on her neck. I asked her how much I should press. She directed me to press more and more, until I was practically pressing her to the floor, exerting a lot of pressure on her neck.

Once her head was on the floor, she spontaneously told me that I was acting like one of her dream figures, a devil who was throwing her into a hole, in a dream. Once she had a clear visualization of the devil pressing her down, once her channels had switched from the pressure to the dream picture, we switched roles and she showed me how the devil pushed her to the floor. After a while the 'devil' said flatly, 'Either you take me with you when you go out or you will have to remain in a hole.' It turned out that she was learning to be more instinctive and honest in public. She was either too sweet or else absent. So I asked her to realize her dreambody work right there and then with me and to be devilishly honest with me about what she liked and disliked. This work then switched into the relationship channel.

In the work we see an interesting aspect of body behavior. Her backache and hand motions were angry reactions to herself because she was not honest, she was too sweet. Her backache was like a dream, a devil, trying to reach consciousness and tell her to be more direct. We could say that her body was dreaming through the medium of the backache. This dream appears in the proprioception of pain and in the double signal of the hand motion. All incompleted motions of the hands and feet are secondary unconscious signals, dream figures trying to express themselves more completely.

Esther's work is an example of working with incomplete hand motions, proprioceptive experience, dialogue and visualization. It is a work in which we see that the body itself creates pain as if it were a devil trying to get Esther to change.

In process work the dream is frequently explained by the

dreamer herself whose understanding is based upon having fully experienced the dreaming process. Interpretation is something which often forces itself upon the dreamer, it is not an intellectual exercise which must be struggled for mentally. Movement and proprioception are the business of the individual dreamer, and can not be organized according to the programs of the therapist. In many cases process work occurs simultaneously with physical healing. But even when this is not the case, body work reveals to the dreamer the meaning of the symptoms; and the experience of what they are trying to achieve.

RUTH'S GOD
Ruth came in complaining of severe headaches. She told me that the doctors wanted to operate on her brain because the computer scans indicated a growth in that area. Recently she has had epileptic seizures. There was a lot of fear expressed with her talk, her face looked like she was in a lot of pain. She told me a 'big dream' in which she met an angel who healed her. In the dream she went up to heaven in a sort of ascension.

The pain in her head got to be so severe while we talked that we switched from talking about the dream to her body experience. There was a great pain in her head, she said, or she put her hand on her head. I put my hand on her head and asked her to direct my hand to the exact place, and to indicate the exact pressure which her body needed.

As we began this 'body' work, I was pressing her head. She asked for more pressure. Then she started to put her own hand on her head again so we switched roles. I asked her to verbalize what she experienced as the 'pressure maker' making pressure on my head. He said, 'Go internal, be still.' After a moment, her pressure disappeared and she felt well. 'Light,' she said. 'I feel light.' Enjoy your ascension,' I said, 'and be quiet.'

In the next hour she began by being meditatively quiet. After a moment her eyes looked up. I asked her what she saw and she said that she saw a child. I told her to look. She moved her shoulders as she described the child, and I noticed this and told her to move like the child. After a moment the child looked upward. I asked her what she saw and she said she saw a loving god. Then, 'Oh, I remember a dream I had in which a child, full of belief, puts its head into the mouth of a threatening dog. Though she is afraid that the child will be eaten, the dog who is at first threatening, becomes loving. The child, dreamer and dog then play together and hug.' After she told me the dream she looked down. I asked her what she then felt. She said she felt like hugging. She said her dream meant that when she believed in God she knew she would not be killed by his rage against her.

The 'child' dream appeared in the midst of the process work and gave Ruth a feeling for the dreaming process and the experience of the dream which she had had. Thus, she understood it herself. The dream gives her a picture of what is trying to happen. In her is a child who naively believes in God and in spirits. This child is protected from the ravenous dog, which she said was a guardian of the gates. I asked her of what gates. 'The gates of God,' she said.

If the child would not believe in God, then the dog would become angry supposedly, and then the dreambody would eat her up. I often observed how death appears as a ravenous animal, in people with cancer, eating up its victims. In this dream, however, the death process had the potential of being reversed, apparently because the 'dog' is angry at her 'child' who believes in spirits. This healing potential was realized and Ruth's health improved.

Here healing, belief, dream and body work are integrated. Visualization was interchanged for proprioception, kinesthesis, then play, renewed memory of a dream and insight, etc. The dreamwork was completed in a way before we heard the dream.

Ruth's primary process was focused upon the life and death situations around her illness. The secondary processes, however, were concerned with the child and the experience of God's power. Process work combines both primary and secondary phenomena by focusing upon the fear of death but also upon the exact nature of the symptoms and their channels.

I make no reference to the explanation or examination of body chemistry or its relationship to dreams. Nor do I attempt to give a final account of what process 'really' is. This phenomenological attitude toward body work is derived from noticing that feedback is best, both in the moment of the work and at a later date, when staying very close to experience and awareness.

It was important to this client that her symptoms radically improved. Thus it was important for me to accept her primary process, her fear of these symptoms as a crucial part of her entire situation. However, it can also be important for the process worker to remember that health and illness are normally cultural concepts belonging mainly to collective definitions and rarely describe a client's secondary processes.

There are indications that a process-oriented approach to the body is beginning to take root in medicine as well as psychology. For example, the physician, Larry Dossey, uses the physicist, David Bohm's, holomovement theory of the universe to show that present concepts of health and disease belong to an outmoded Newtonian era.[1] According to Dossey, 'the body behaves more as a pattern and process than as an isolated and non interacting object. It cannot be localized in space and its boundary is essentially illusory.[2] And later, 'Connected as we are to all other bodies, comprised as we are of an unending flux of events themselves occurring in spacetime, we regard ourselves not as bodies fixed in time at particular points, but as eternally changing patterns for which precise descriptive terms seem utterly inappropriate.'[3] (pp. 142-9)

Dossey's concept of the body reflects the theory in physics that an 'implicate order' exists which manifests itself in 'explicate phenomena'[4] by 'enfolding' itself through the work of some perceiver. Thus process-oriented psychology is a concrete realization of the physicist's theory, one method of allowing dreaming or implicit order to unravel itself through the awareness, discipline and courageousness of the observer.

Practical reality, however, requires the process worker,

interested in perceiving and 'enfolding' 'implicate orders,' to have a wide range of experience and as much knowledge about 'subjective' human signals as possible. It is difficult to convey the precise nature of these signals on paper because many are non-verbal and because discipline is required to pick them up. Practical demonstration, personal experience, training seminars and the use of video equipment are useful aids in developing this discipline.[5] A very rough estimate of the amount of detailed knowledge required to pick up these signals predicts that knowledge of over five hundred commonly occurring body motions, gestures, facial expressions, hand motions, eye movements and breaths as well as an innumerable number of language constructions is required to achieve sufficient contact with a client's dream and body processes. And when these signals and methods of working with them are mastered, unknown channels and processes always seem to appear to humble the elation of first successes.

# Chapter 4
# RELATIONSHIP CHANNELS

One of the client's most complex and central channels is the therapist himself. The relationship between two people is called transference, which Freud originally meant to connote the projection of infantile problems onto the therapist. Jung took transference processes out of the Freudian, reductive setting and showed with the use of alchemical symbolism just how the transference implied not only the projection of family figures but also a host of other images such as the shaman, the wise old man or woman, the divine child and the great witch onto the therapist.[1] Jung indicated how relationship problems such as those which occurred during analysis took place in a collective 'bath', a milieu in which one could no longer divide the therapist's individuation process, his complexes and conscious problems from those of the so-called patient.

Relationship appears differently in different psychologies. Gestalt's Fritz Perls spoke of 'confluence', the flowing together of two individuals in such a way that the processes of the one became indistinguishable from the other.[2] For Perls relationship was a process of differentiating personal from collective events creating and destroying boundaries.[3]

Transactional analysis defines relationships in familiar terms such as parent-child, adult-adult and child-child.[4] Modern neuro-linguistic programmers practice Freudian theory in so far as personal relationships between the individual and therapist are avoided because they create dependence.[5] Behavioral therapists also avoid the trans-

ference as an unnecessary part of counseling.[6] Jung indicated some of the possible reasons why the therapists avoid
the transference.[7] He says that therapists crawl behind their
shields as doctor and healer when they have not worked
through certain problems and when they are therefore in
danger of falling into affects such as loving, hating and
getting turned on or off by the patient. Such therapists
develop methods partially in order to avoid their own
affects. Sitting behind a desk or method is essentially the
same; both shield one from the onslaught of projections,
and unpredictable processes.

DREAMED-UP PROCESSES
The transference is complicated by the confusing situation in
which there are two human beings interacting with one
another as two inextricably coupled systems which simultaneously behave as if they were one process. Every time a
dreamer tells a dream, the dream interpreter typically has
reactions to the dreamer, which dream figures have towards
the dreamer himself. These reactions occur before, during
and even after the dream is told. The reactions of the
therapist are 'dreamed up' so to speak by the dreamer.

For example, a dreamer who has difficulty appreciating
herself invariably dreams up real people to love her and
dream figures to care for her. A man who is blown up out of
proportions about his abilities, dreams up police to hold him
down and therapists who cut him down. A woman who is
unconscious of her own power gets into violent fights in her
dreams and manages to practically destroy a battery of
therapists. Yet she still feels weak.

Dreamers in need of body awareness dreaming of sex and
contact, dream up body therapists and massage techniques.
In other words, specific therapies can be dreamed up by the
dreamer without the therapist ever realizing that the reason
his method works is because it is the dreamer's process.
Most therapists rarely consider that their therapies and
reactions are subject to the dreamer's dream-field or that
they could be the creations of a collective unconsciousness.

I do not want to go into the mechanics of dreaming up

here as they are mentioned elsewhere.[8] Suffice it to say that the majority of dreamed-up reactions occur because the therapist has not consciously picked up the client's double signals and therefore reacts to them without even realizing what his reactions are due to. These double body signals are dreamlike, they are unconscious to the client and call forth communications and reactions in the therapist just as they call forth similar reactions in the client's dreams. However, there are some situations which are parapsychological in the sense that people can be dreamed up at such a distance that double signals cannot be spoken of. These dreamed-up phenomena have no simple causal explanations in terms of visual, auditory or proprioceptive communication based upon the speed of light, of sound waves, or of electro-magnetic fields.

The central point of the present discussion is that phenomenologically speaking we must conclude that many of the therapist's so-called counter-transference reactions to his client are dreamed up, that is they belong primarily to the dreamer's process and can be located there in terms of his dream figures. The therapist has unwittingly become an expression or channel of the client's process, a channel carrying signals and messages which the client is not aware of in himself and which he may not care to become aware of. The therapist becomes a part, so to speak, of the client's dreambody.

*An example*

Consider the situation of a client of one of my students. She had been complaining to him for months that she was plagued by feelings of self-hatred, without getting to the bottom of these feelings or changing them. It seemed as if her negative dream figures had been dreamed up in the environment and she now experienced unbearable hatred from her friends. My student admitted to me that he too was beginning to dislike her, without knowing why. He showed me a video-tape of a discussion with her and we soon found the problem. He began to dislike her when she sent out signals of inflation. In other words, his negative feelings were dreamed-up reactions to her signals of inflation. As soon as he realized this he understood himself to be a channel for her dreaming process, and could sympathize more completely with her negative dream figures. They came into being together with their dreamed-up counterparts in this woman's reality in order to balance her inflation.

### PROJECTION AND DREAMING UP

As long as the therapist has a reaction which is short-lived and lasts only as long as he is in the vicinity of the client, we can speak of a purely dreamed-up reaction. If, however, this reaction lasts longer than the time of the interview, or if it was present even before the session, we must also consider the possibility that the therapist is unconsciously projecting something of himself onto his client in addition to being simultaneously dreamed up by the client.

Projection may be differentiated from dreaming up. If the therapist has a strong reaction to the dreamer which is long lasting and which cannot be found in the dreamer's dream or body work, then we must assume that the therapist has a projection onto the client, which belongs primarily to the therapist. We speak of dreaming up when the therapist has no affects before, after or as soon as the dreamer has integrated and understood his dream material.

Relationship processes are complicated by the fact that dreaming up and projecting often happen simultaneously in both parties. For example, a therapist may feel that his client should be developing more feeling while the client resists this change because he feels it is not right for him. The client dreams that he is plagued by a negative figure who is trying to make him into a feeling person while the therapist dreams about developing more feeling. Here, the therapist has become a negative figure for the client while the client has become a negative dream figure for the therapist who himself is in need of more feeling. Both are projecting and dreaming each other up!

**WORKING WITH DREAMING UP**
Process science thus empirically discovers that the therapist can be a channel for the client and vice versa. Since process work proceeds by amplifying the strongest signal occupying the foreground of awareness, if the therapist's reactions prevail, then these reactions must be amplified until processes begin. His reaction may then unleash something in the client who may then enter into his dream process more completely.

As soon as the therapist's process is incorporated into the work, therapy changes as roles such as doctor-patient, healer-healee disappear temporarily while process creates and annhilates, rebuilding the relationship on a firmer groundwork than before.

If relationship is not allowed to transform into a process, work becomes rigid and boring. The patient then frequently and correctly accuses the therapist of misunderstanding or authoritarianism while the therapist devises some sort of lame excuse for dismissing his client's reactions.

**RESPONSIBILITY**
The idea of projection places most psychological responsibility for affective processes upon the person making the projection and secondarily upon the individual who may and usually does have some sort of little 'hook' for this projection.[9] 'Dreaming up' places responsibility upon both parties. In the extreme case in which the therapist has nothing in his dreams reflecting the client's behavior and in which the client dreams of the therapist's affects, we must put responsibility for relationship problems upon the dreamer, even if he is a passive and apparent victim of the therapist's emotions.

I have been speaking of the client as if he is the dreamer. The reader should realize, however, that the therapist can also dream up strong love and hate reactions from the client, the so-called transference, simply because the therapist either loves himself insufficiently or because he possesses inadequate self-criticism.

## CONTROLLED ABANDON

It takes courage to let yourself be a potential channel for someone else. Someone will always argue against 'letting things happen,' expressing reactions and abandoning the normal therapeutic framework in which a therapeutic program determines more or less what happens. For example, the argument goes that letting in the therapist's unconscious will swamp the dreamer or present him with a reaction he is not ready to receive.

## CAUSALITY IN RELATIONSHIP

In a world where projection and dreaming up occur, we can say that every signal causes everything or that causality is insignificant. In other words people have not caused your problems but have rather become channels for your process—or vice versa.

In Diagram 3, pictures 1 and 2, we see how the dreamer may dream up the world of which the therapist is part, just as the therapist can dream up a client. Since, however, one person is not usually dreamed up by another without having some sort of unconsciousness, we have to consider two or more interacting dream fields as in picture 3. Since we cannot say to whom a dream belongs we can add the effect of two or more dream fields and arrive at picture 4. Here you see one field whose center is nowhere or rather at infinity. This implies that both dreamer and interpreter are part of a universal process, which uses both people as channels.

*An example*

An interesting demonstration of primary and secondary processes, projection, dreaming up and the universal field is reflected in Ruth's relationship with her husband David. David and Ruth have come to me because they are in the midst of a four- or five-month long battle. Ruth yells wildly that David has no respect for her interest in quietness and privacy. According to Ruth, David is a wild and exciting but insensitive person who in his profession as an entertainer and as a man at home is capable of waking up the dead.

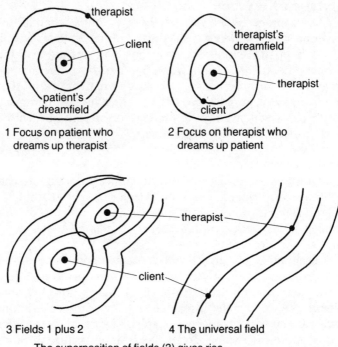

1 Focus on patient who
dreams up therapist

2 Focus on therapist who
dreams up patient

3 Fields 1 plus 2

4 The universal field

The superposition of fields (3) gives rise
to a universal field (4) without center.

*Diagram 3*

David, who doesn't notice her wild yelling, can hardly
understand what Ruth is talking about. He claims that he is
decent and quiet at home and has no interest in disturbing
anybody for any reason whatsoever. Ruth's primary process
and David's primary process are both being quiet and
decent. Ruth's secondary process is projected onto David.
Her secondary process is being wild, insensitive, noisy,
exciting and tense.

The reason that I say that she projects this upon him is
because when I asked her to play him she jumped up and
down, ran around, and was excited, noisy and insensitive,
naturally hoping while she was playing to provoke him and
to make fun of him. However, when I asked her to meditate

upon her behavior while she was doing it she said in fact that she herself was the way she had described David when she is without him in public. There she experiences herself as trying to get the center of attention, jumping around, being wild, exciting and full of tension. As the conversation between David and Ruth proceeded she acted extremely sensitively and quietly, sitting in her chair as prim and pretty as could be. The quieter and more decently she behaved in her conversation with David, the wilder and more impossible he seemed to become. David was being dreamed up to behave like her secondary process in part because she has too little relationship to this process. He is being provoked to compensate for her one-sidedness.

On the other hand, when David was alone, sitting and talking to me in another session, he tended himself to behave as he described himself, quietly, sensitively and related to what was happening. However, in one of the dreams he told me, Ruth was just as wild as could be. Naturally he was surprised by this dream because he does not see either her wild double signals or his own wildness. Thus we could say that he dreams her up to be wild and insensitive in part because he himself has little awareness of this side of himself, since he has more contact than she with wildness and he doesn't project it yet or have psychosomatic symptoms around it. So here's a case in which projection and dreaming up were happening in both partners simultaneously. I'm not going to say more about them right now, more about their history or how I worked with them, because I want to center simply upon the processes of dreaming up and projecting and the common field between them. This dream field is organized by the polarity between decency and wildness. Both David and Ruth are channels for a common dream-field process which is not caused by anyone!

### THE UNIVERSAL DREAM FIELD
A process view of relationships gives us a noncausal, final perspective which sees them as aspects of a field of Jung's collective unconscious or as subjective impressions of a

universal Tao or archetypical process. A dream field is to psychology as Einstein's master field is to physics. Analogically speaking, each of us is an especially intense or condensed point in a field with dream dimensions. We are each channels for a universal Tao or process.

Actually this argument may be valid. It creates a powerful objection to group therapy, for example, in which people are encouraged to criticize others without reservation. Indeed, simply letting out a reaction can be potentially dangerous, for it can release a psychic avalanche or even a psychosis. The overly zealous therapist must realize that his reactions will usually be automatically integrated in time by his client even if these reactions are *not* expressed—if he is patient enough to wait for the dreamer to discover things on his own.

Therapists either liberally react to their clients or else repress their reactions. The theory of dreaming up, however, shows that both reactions are insufficient. Reactions released without any control whatsoever will be rejected even if they belong to the unconscious of the other person precisely because they are unconscious! Hence violent or uncontrolled reactions are met with equally violent and uncontrolled resistances.

However, repressing the therapist's reactions is no better because repression is an illusion. You can not repress dreaming up because it is not controllable. Repressed reactions only look repressed. The therapy scene under the domination of an even mildly repressive framework only looks orderly. Precise observation indicates that repressed reactions become somatized in the form of double signals and body problems, they make the therapist an incongruent, ill and unconvincing physician.

### THE BODY IN THE THERAPEUTIC RELATIONSHIP

Each of us knows what it is like to be dreamed up physically. How 'uptight' or nervous we feel in certain people's neighborhood. How we get stomach cramps, headaches and other symptoms apparently in reaction to someone's behavior. These same reactions appear in therapists along with strong physical signals such as being exhausted by a dreamer, being turned on or off sexually by him, getting cramps, becoming nervous, suddenly becoming happy or sad, etc.

The average student therapist will, after some hesitation, bring in dreamed-up emotions such as anger, fear, hatred, love and boredom. But interacting physically out of a sudden need to touch, kiss, press, pull, hit, stab, kick, hug, love, sleep, walk, move, pinch or play is a different matter. We have culturally oriented inhibitions about body communication.

In addition to cultural inhibitions there are a host of personal reservations to body contact, some of which are a combination of psychic and physical resistances. Some people must resist close body contact because they are in danger of losing their own process. They feel obliged to focus only upon the needs of the other person during such contact and hence experience physical contact as a sort of death. For them contact is dangerous and must be avoided until they can bring their own physical needs to life.

There are other types of therapists who are so starved for body contact that they avoid it in order to save themselves from their exaggerated longings. These therapists have unworked-out problems and would be well advised to work more on themselves.

Some therapists do not touch people because they feel this would invade the other person's territory. Naturally there are moments when contact could truly be an invasion. However, consistent avoidance looks more like a symptom of someone who is projecting their own lack of boundaries than a true appreciation of the other's privacy. In other words the therapist fearful of invasion is too easily invaded by others himself. I should also mention that the therapist's hesitations may also be dreamed up and are part of a relationship process. If the therapist gets suddenly shy, it is possible that the client is hiding something!

### SEX AS A DREAMED-UP REACTION

A therapist or anyone else whose physical functioning is limited dreams up the environment to become turned on or to enter directly into physical contact with them. Naturally getting sexually turned on to someone may be dreamed up by many other circumstances also. People who are hiding something turn you on in order to open them up. People who do not love themselves turn you on to love them. People who have cramps and diseases of the genital area turn you on to work out the problems there. Dying people can turn you on to bring them to life. People with beautiful bodies stimulate others if they do not have enough self-appreciation. Head trippers bait you to turn off their heads.

Being sexually dreamed up is often accompanied by physical and fantasiful resistances, the latter being projected onto partners or therapy systems. The typical fantasies are 'what will my partner think, how will the other person's partner feel? Is this therapy? Will someone see what I am doing?' These spontaneous fantasy invaders may appear at the moment of contact and do not belong to consciousness because they cannot be controlled. They are 'bona fide' unconscious processes seeking an amplification. Some of these contents turn out to be negative mothers and fathers, for example, who, like priests, are asking for enlightenment about sex. Other uninvited guests reveal themselves as protectors guarding against confluent invasion of personal territory.

I remember a student who got turned on by a woman and followed his body, pressing her with his back to the wall. Suddenly his excitement abated as she came out with the following story. Years ago she had been exposed to an exhibitionist who had paralyzed her with fear. At that time she could not move or defend herself. As soon as she realized what story she was telling she defended herself and told the student to move away. In other words she had dreamed up the past traumatic invasion of privacy and the present one because she herself needed to learn how to make boundaries.

## SEXUAL CONTACT AND MALPRACTICE COMPLAINTS

The growing need for malpractice insurance especially among American physicians and psychotherapists seems also to be an aspect of dreaming up. The patient who is in need of or who is afraid of physical contact brings with him or herself an inner judge, a police court and a jury. As this client nears the therapist, the jury usually takes the foreground of the interaction and relationship is bound to be formal and social. As the two get to know each other, resistances are bound to take the background as the real needs come up. The beginning therapist often feels guilty and surprised about his own fear and social rigidity, and frequently jumps over this dreamed-up stiffness into physical contact with his patient. The typical client is at first pleased and then overcome by the unintegrated hesitation, the jury and court. The client is pressed from within to bring the therapist before an outer jury and his inner life is lived out in a courtroom.

This malpractice experience can be integrated as part of the relationship work. The therapist must bring in his uptight reactions saying, 'Sorry, I am interested, but not in you, I do not trust you, do not really know you, I do not feel your dream figures have all been brought in, your hesitations are still there, I am busy with someone else . . . etc.' The very attempt to discuss the situation takes the relationship phenomenon out of the somatic channels and allows what is happening to express itself verbally, the main channel for most western couples, and the one which can therefore be used to integrate what is happening into experiences of everyday life. When the jury and court are brought into the session, it seems as if very few relationship interactions have purely sexual characteristics.

## RELIGIOUS ASPECTS OF CONTACT

If we wish to understand the dreamed-up nature of sexuality or the meaning of becoming a physical channel for someone we have to leave our cultural myths and look elsewhere to see how other people have attempted to integrate sexuality.

Indian practitioners of Tantra yoga[10] and Chinese Taoist alchemists[11] ritualized sexual contact, seeing it as the basic state from which religious experiences are derived. In Tantra, sexual contact is slowed down until it is almost stopped. Hatha yoga is then practiced in order to drive the sexual impulse out of the genital area, through the spine and into the entire body encouraging it to perform spontaneous postures which awaken somatic consciousness to the point of nirvanic experience. The Tantra yogi sees sex as one means for reaching a god experience and as a method for knowing this god as himself in contact with the goddess of the partner.

The Taoist uses the partner of the opposite sex as a stimulant for his 'mercury,' his 'prima materia,' the basic substance to be transformed into the 'panacea' for health and long life.[12] He captures his sexual stimulation and meditates upon it, 'circulating' its 'fire,' from the genitals into the stomach, heart and mind plexi and around through his back. The transformed and circulated substance becomes, through meditation, an immortal being or the so-called subtle body; the individual himself existing outside of normal consciousness.

A comparative study of these religious rituals gives us some idea of the possible archetypical pattern behind sexuality. Tantric and Taoist rituals 'work on' sex as if it were a basic condition leading to something else. They do not experience sexuality as a simple 'just-so-fact' or state but as a process which is trying to evolve. In the language of process theory, sex turns on proprioceptive channels which ritual then switches into vision and enlightenment. The transformation of sex into a 'higher energy' implies that what we call sex is only a presage of something which has relatively little to do with genital stimulation. Sex is one of many body states.

In so far as rituals transform sex into subtle body altered states of consciousness, sex is no different than any other body signal. All signals are signs of 'Shakti'[13] that is of god or of the the inner guides of the unconscious. All autonomous body signals create the sensation of an unpredictable spirit of life, requiring amplification in order to reveal its true nature.

## ON THE SIGNIFICANCE OF DIFFERENT THEORIES

The concept of dreaming up makes it possible for us to appreciate very different kinds of therapists and therapy forms from a new angle. There is no one absolute theory that can be good for everyone, because a given person in a certain process dreams up a particular form of therapist. Thus therapists who are zealously involved in breaking through their clients' resistances are dreamed up by the fearful, mistrusting aspects of our culture. Overly conservative, head-oriented therapies are needed by people who are too loose, and in need of reflection. In one sense the power struggles between different schools of psychiatry, social work and psychology are irrelevant because different clients need different forms of therapy. Moreover, different cultures require different types of 'medicine men'. What we need is greater understanding of the common process and flexibility in different schools and therapists, not an annihilation of them.

## RELATIONSHIP TO THE COLLECTIVE

One of the interesting conclusions of dreaming up is that you can become sick because of a given collective situation. Just as an acute symptom can be constellated in the neighborhood of someone who is not living his unconscious, a chronic disease may come from a culture which has rigidified. It is possible, for example, that much suffering related to presently intractable diseases such as cancer balances the personal, familial and cultural tendency of western people to avoid pain.

In primitive societies the relationship between collective and individual diseases appears in rituals where the shaman routinely requires the entire family or even tribes to partake in a given healing. I understand such rituals better after having been at body seminars. I never fail to be amazed at how physically relieving it is for everyone if one person lives a body or fantasy system. On the other hand, it is very stressful to be in a public situation which represses somatic channels and signals.

If you consider dreaming up then you can no longer innocently feel that a collective or individual has done something to you. Such causual thinking no longer holds. If you direct your attention with precision to your own dreams and to the dreams of your partners, you are bound to get a glimpse of the objective pattern behind what is happening. The important questions are no longer 'who is doing what?' but 'what is trying to happen?'

Causal attitudes towards dreaming up and towards relationship problems are natural, unconscious but almost always opposed by negative feedback from the environment. The very attempt at explaining to someone that they have dreamed you up or that you have dreamed them up always contains an element of blame because of the presence of the causal belief that the dreamer is 'doing' something. Dreaming up is a noncausal phenomenon, it is an aspect of a field whose localities are not connected through direct causal interchange alone.

Thus, though blaming and causal accusations are normal aspects of relationship phenomena, closer study of the secondary processes behind relationships indicates that an implicit or dream-like order is trying to enfold by means of individual lives.

Thus an individual can be considered as the unconscious or the split-off and dreamed-up part of another person or group just as the group can be understood as a part of the individual. If we switch our viewpoints and no longer consider the individual and his dream as the center of the universe, but the universe's process as the central phenomenon organizing the behavior of its individual parts, we enter that part of psychology which borders upon relativistic physics.

# Chapter 5
# WORLD CHANNELS

When objects and distant localities of spacetime behave as if they belonged to an individual's process as in *déjà vu*, telepathy and other forms of synchronicity, we can speak of the world as if it were a channel for the dreamer. Synchronicity is a generalization of dreaming up but differs from it insofar as we can not say empirically that the inorganic environment is dreaming up the individual in the same way as a dreamer might be understood as doing this. Though the empirical nature of the environment's 'dreaming' or implicate order may be different from that of a human being's, still the phenomenon of dreaming up gives us the feeling of how matter might 'feel' or experience itself as a part of our dream field.

The relationship between physics and psychology is nowhere as intimate as in the phenomena Jung called synchronicity though in principle the entire realm of psychology may be considered an aspect of physics and vice versa. One of the advantages of process science is its neutral basis. Since process work is based upon a phenomenological viewpoint, terms such as psyche and matter, inner and outer, psychology and physics, are replaced by the experiences, awareness and observations of a given observer. Thus the physicist's approach to 'purely material' events is, in principle, no different than the process worker's approach to body, dream, or relationship experiences.

It seems that the revolution now taking place in physics[1] is erasing the dividing line between that science and its reflections in psychology and mythology.[2] Physicists too have been testing the tyrannical nature of causal thinking and casting doubts upon the validity of our most commonplace notions of the world. After more than three thousand years of searching for the most elementary particles and principles of nature, scientists now consider the idea of atoms illusory. The most modern thinkers realize that physical theory is a reflection of the human personality.

Einstein's relativity theory, Bell's theorem and empirical investigations in physics force us to consider that objects and events can communicate with each other across great distances without apparent signal exchange.[3] The possibility of such communication disturbed physicists such as Einstein who held that a certain reasonableness about nature must be insisted upon. Even though Einstein upset our notions of space and time with his relativity theory, he rigidly held that a universe could not exist in which such events as telepathy and telekinesis could take place even though such events are permitted by the breakdown of the principle of local causes.[4] According to this principle events in a given locality are influenced only by that locality and not by signals from events at distances which would require signals to travel faster than the speed of light.

The breakdown of causality in the quantum world and the existence of signals traveling faster than the speed of light have shaken the conventional western logic and supplemented it with what the physicists call 'quantum logic.' This new way of thinking is close to process work and may be used in part to understand post-Einsteinian phenomena or processes occurring in world channels.

ONE-WORLD CONCEPTS
This new logic is based upon the experimentability of events in contrast to preconceived notions about them. The new logic implies, for physicists such as David Bohm, the existence of a 'one world.'[5] This one-world theory of the universe mirrors Buddhist concepts which rule out separate or independent localities. In the Buddhist's universe all events behave in conjunction with all other events, creating

one larger universal process.

The one-world concept is occurring also to biologists such as Lewis Thomas.[6] Starting with the behavior of large groups of individual animals such as ants, he speculates that our entire planet behaves basically like a single cell in which each of us functions in a way which can be best understood by looking at the events of the entire world.

One-world concepts are found as well in analytical psychology. Jung theorized early in this century about the existence of a sort of field which he called the collective unconscious which can be seen reflected in the dreams of individuals at any given time. Already in the 1950s, Jung, together with the physicist Wolfgang Pauli, postulated something very close to quantum logic in order to explain telepathy and other parapsychological events. Jung said that events like telepathy which could not be entirely explained in terms of some sort of cause, could nevertheless be accounted for by a noncausal principle which he called synchronicity.[7] This principle has a strong Taoist flavor about it, and implies the existence of a meaningful order which pervades a given timespace.[8] For example the Tao, or prevailing meaning, would be a possible connecting factor between a dream, a hexagram of the I Ching pulled the same morning, and a real event mirroring the dream and I Ching occurring that afternoon.

We can guess that there is a common thread connecting physical concepts such as quantum logic, one-world theory, the principle of local causes and psychological ideas such as the collective unconscious and synchronicity. This thread leads us to suspect a meeting ground between the two sciences, physics and psychology. However, approaching this common ground is made difficult by the fact that physicists tend to be unfamiliar with psychological processes just as psychologists may be unaware of the theory and problems of physics. Nevertheless, attempts are being made to bridge the sciences.[9] In this present chapter I want to continue to investigate the common ground and in particular to show how the discoveries of process science give empirical weight to the notions of physics and how psychology is already living the one world of processes which physics is talking about.

### DREAM AND BODY WORK

Let's turn to psychophysical processes in psychology in order to investigate post-Einsteinian signals. I recall one especially interesting synchronicity occurring during dream work. During one of my dream seminars a man began to tell a dream about a bear. Just as he was saying, 'and then the bear appeared,' in walked a man through the door of the seminar room, a man called Bear. Mr Bear told us that he was held up on his way to the seminar and could not maintain his normally punctual behavior.

The two events, namely the telling of the dream in which the bear appeared and the coming of Mr Bear have no simple causal connection, no ordinary electromagnetic signal connection which we can imagine (besides that is, some sort of magical causality). Of course we can consider the two counts as accidents, but the dreamer, his dream and seminar participants had strong emotional reactions to the events indicating that a theory of pure chance would deny or even repress the total reality of the observations. Ideas such as a theory of non-local causes, superluminal communications or synchronicity would be more appropriate here because the observers experienced the events as communicating with one another or as being connected by some sort of order.

Instead of analyzing this situation in detail, I would like to tell about a second synchronicity which took place during a body seminar. A participant was trying to lift up a very heavy object at one point during this seminar, allowing his body energy to express itself in the way it wanted. Falling backwards, exhausted by the impossibility of his task, the man exclaimed in an emotional tone that he felt that the object he was trying to lift was a god, something which he could not and was not meant to overcome.

As he was pronouncing his discovery there was a knock on the door of the seminar room. (It must be mentioned that this knock was surprising to us because the seminar was taking place in the high mountains where visitors were very rare.) We opened the door and in marched three children dressed up as the three kings of Bethlehem who, together with their great star were pointing the way towards god. They sang their songs (looking at the dreamer) turned and left. The atmosphere was so loaded that as soon as they disappeared people became very emotional, feeling that somehow god had been in the room. The day of the synchronicity was the 6th of January, the day in that Swiss mountain town when the children acted out the three kings' ritual. However, the children normally only acted out their rituals in the villages. Their very appearance high in the alps and at the exact moment of the man's enlightenment seemed to be non-chance events.

An interesting aspect of this synchronicity contrasts it to the bear story. In the bear synchronicity, everyone was shocked. In the god synchronicity everyone except the dreamer was shocked. In fact he said that he almost expected it to happen. He experienced the events as coherent and as agreements with his state partly because he had dreamed that he had lost a fight with god the night before and partly because he was in that special dream state because of the body work.

Why were the reactions of the dreamers in the bear and god synchronicities so different? What do these reactions say about the relationships between the observer and events? Can we imagine superluminal signals (i.e. faster than the speed of light) between events, or a post-Einsteinian universe where all is connected? What does process science tell us about the physicist's one world and psychologist's synchronicities?

We recall from the discussions in chapter 3 that proprioceptive experience is patterned visually by dreams and that the latter may be found in body symptoms when amplified. The invariance between dream and body processes gives rise to the dreambody concept.[10] In chapter 4 we discovered that the dreamer's environment behaves like specific dream activities, or that the world around him is 'dreamed up.' Dreaming up gave rise to the concept of the universal dream field which means that the body phenomena and exterior situations which one notices as disturbances are aspects of one's own dream process. Synchronicities indicate that the inorganic world as well as the human environment can also behave in dream-like fashion.

## PROCESS LOGIC

The natural question which now arises is, of course, what the nature of the dream field is like. Phenomenological theory makes no attempt at answering this question unless empirical evidence arises, demonstrating either causally oriented signal-receiver phenomena or superluminal signals. Process science works with the facts of perception. These facts may be used to answer the following questions. Is there a sort of dream logic corresponding to a quantum logic? Are the dream field, the dreambody and the irrational aspect of quantum physics organized by some unknown pattern?

As we have previously seen, dream work indicates that outer events are not haphazard phenomena, but conform to patterns and have meanings. The course of inner and outer processes conforms to the patterns or archetypes found in the dreams of the observer. These patterns create the essence of process, 'process logic.' This logic gives coherence to all spontaneous perceptions. For example, apparently dissociated dream fragments are not independent pieces of some chaos, but cluster around a particular archetype. Jung called this archetype the 'architect' of dreams.[11]

For example, in the first story the man with the bear dream was living in a dream world architected by the archetypal image of the bear which organized his body processes, synchronicities and relationships. The second man who fought with god was living in a dream world structured by the archetypal fight with god, a dream term for the process which was drawing the dreamer towards religious experiences and enlightenment and organizing 'outer' synchronistic events.

## ARCHETYPES AND WAVE FUNCTIONS

Now if we are exact, then we can not call archetypes by dream names such as the bear or god because these are too static. Archetypal patterns are processes or rather tendencies for these processes to happen. A dream report, for example, describes a certain tendency. For example, in the bear synchronicity, there was a tendency towards the process of meeting a great force. The dream report coinciding with the god synchronicity described a tendency towards conflict, humility and enlightenment.

Process-oriented dream and body work shows that dream images and symptoms are the beginning of tendencies towards particular psycho-physical processes. One can outline these tendencies by using entire dreams or body experiences mirroring these dreams.[12] In process work one sees these tendencies amplify and actualize themselves, creating body expressions, fantasies, understanding and synchronicities.

Now we have seen that the empirical universe which the process worker observes may be called a dream universe, described and oriented not only by the reasonable and commonplace logic of ordinary consciousness, but also by archetypal tendencies towards processes. They may appear in body problems, relationship conflicts, dream and syn-chronicities, in proprioceptive channels or referred channels such as people or outer objects.

Now it is just these tendencies which connect psychology to physics. The physicist has described the world since the early part of this century in terms of quantum mechanical tendencies. Physics had to drop normal ways of describing events in terms of elementary images such as atoms, time and space. It was discovered that what happens in the sub-atomic realm of being could only be accounted for by certain probabilistic equations, which, because they also describe wave phenomena in the real world, were called wave equations. The probabilistic interpretation of these wave equations caused physicists great problems. At first they were upset and baffled by the idea that a mathematical probability function described reality more accurately than a one-to-one cause and effect connection between events and theories. Quantum mechanics created religious conflicts for Einstein judging by his famous statement to Bohr that the god of the physical universe could not be probabilistic and 'play with dice.'[13]

After debates which are still going on today, the majority of physicists finally settled upon the so-called Copenhagen interpretation of the wave equation which says that it tells us about the probabilities and tendencies for things to happen. In the words of Werner Heisenberg who was greatly responsible for formulating the 'new' physics, the wave equation was

> . . . a tendency for something. It was a quantitative version of the old concept of 'potentia' in Aristotelian philosophy. It introduced something standing in the middle between the idea of an event and the actual event, a strange kind of physical reality just in the middle between possibility and reality.[14]

The lack of clarity about this 'strange kind of physical reality,' has led some scientists to project Buddhist thought into the formulation of physics. The one-world experiences of meditation and the pervading reality of the 'atman' fill the intellectual gaps created by the post-Einsteinian world of non-local causes. According to some, language itself can no longer be used in describing this world because the world can only be experienced.[15]

If, however, we compare the Copenhagen interpretation of the wave functions as 'a tendency for something' or of Heisenberg's 'potentia' with the idea of the archetype as a tendency towards certain processes, we are forced to a conclusion. The physicist's wave function is a mathematical aspect of the tendencies the psychologist calls archetypes. The physicist's one world then corresponds to dream world, and other terms used to describe the world of tendencies.

Jung used medieval expressions to describe this one world. He said with the alchemists that the 'Unus Mundus,'[16] was the one world which existed before the first day of creation. Jung meant that this world can be experienced but not grasped, that it is the vessel of preconscious contents, a world which he later termed the 'psychoid unconscious.'[17] The Unus Mundus is the world of archetypes in contrast to the world of archetypal manifestations such as dream processes and synchronicities.

Von Franz has extended Jung's idea of the Unus Mundus into the world of mathematics. She defined the substratum from which ordinary integers arise as the 'one continuum.'[18] Each number is an elementary unit which carries the quality of the one continuum with it as well as a differentiable aspect which makes it an individual number. The one continuum or Unus Mundus reflects a level of existence from which the manifest world is created, a level physicists such as David Finkelstein would define as 'a primitive concept of process' which comes before space and time.[19] As far as I can see, in our culture this level of existence refers to nonvisual proprioceptive awareness.

### DETACHED OBSERVATION VS EXPERIENCE

The various one-world formulations of the dream universe are based upon a standard reference frame, our ordinary chronological reality. As long as we sit in this framework we experience the dream universe in terms of this framework, namely in terms of static states and differentiated descriptions such as tendencies towards specific processes. From this framework we can speak of process logic and of the patterns which are trying to occur in the form of processes.

Process differs from the other one-world descriptions of the dream-world universe in that process implies the experience of dreams and body phenomena. Process describes the observer's experience of the flow of events in which he is now taking part after having temporarily left his static rigid framework while process logic refers to observations of an observer standing with a chronological frame of reference. Wave functions, 'strange physical realities,' post-Einsteinian signals, the Unus Mundus psychoid unconscious, are important aspects of process logic which describe observation as a classical observer in consensus reality.

Process, however, implies detachment and involvement in these archetypal tendencies, which manifest in specific channels.

## THE OBSERVER'S PSYCHOLOGY

We have seen how the one world of physics described by wave functions is similar to the dream world and its archetypal tendencies. We saw how the descriptions of this world in terms of tendencies is organized by process logic and depends upon the observer's frame of reference. This frame of reference defines his psychology.

For example, if at a given time and place an observer genuinely feels no emotional involvement with whatever he may be experiencing then the world he is observing is one in which chance, probability and non-sense may be ruling. Of course, the fact that he is observing anything at all may require some minimal emotional involvement. But just now I am describing a limiting case, an extreme situation of minimal emotional participation.

If, however, the observer finds himself emotionally touched by whatever he is seeing, hearing or feeling, he becomes involved in a totally new situation which is oriented by emotions, projections, dreams and archetypal tendencies. The universe becomes a dream world governed by the patterns of processes.

We may differentiate several typical ways which observers use to relate to the dream world determining to some extent the way in which subsequent processes evolve.[20] For example, there is the chronological observer who talks about processes as tendencies. He may look at manifestations of these processes in dreams and body problems, he may intellectualize about them, but he does not get into them. He maintains his normal intellectual consciousness, keeps his distance from the tendencies he subtly experiences and does not let go of his normal consciousness or give himself even in part to the tendencies which he feels are around.

The chronological observer therefore tells us that the dream world is a 'strange world,' a foreign universe. Personally he may be overcome by this world in a dream or by an emotion. He may feel it pressing upon him as an enemy in the form of a difficult disease or feel spooked by this world. He maintains the position of a Newtonian scientist in a classical space and time framework. He may be a rational person who appreciates and supports the conventions and doings of his reality, finding the other world 'a separate reality,' a 'para' phenomena, a body with a disease, a dream from out of the blue, a person giving him trouble, but not as an aspect of himself. Dreams are dreams, diseases are diseases, and reality is reality for him. He himself is whoever he standardly identifies himself to be. The world is a staccato series of movements between static states.

We can define another observer's relationship to processes, the fluid ego. When this person feels a tendency trying to happen in his body, in a conversation, or a fantasy, he lets himself change, moving into the body experience, mood, or fantasy. The fluid ego is more flexible than the chronological observer who relates everything to his time and space, seeing the world in a solid, frozen static state. The fluid ego lets go of his identification with time, space and cultural tradition, with his conscious intent and primary processes. He temporarily lets his definition of himself and the world stop and experiences its tendencies and strangeness as part of himself. He steps over his edges, follows his secondary processes, guided by momentary experiences and not by a prearranged reality program. When this person gets sick or has trouble with his world he experiences his body and world as a dreambody or dream-world process, not as a disease or outer problem but as something which he is trying to express. Conflicts in relationships are battles he is having with himself, moods are gradients and paths along which he may temporarily choose to move. He becomes an unpredictable and mercurial person who lives in one world, participating in it as if it were him and as if he were one of its vital parts. He does not observe synchronicities but feels processes occurring in outer channels and experiences events as 'agreements,' of his path.[21]

A chronological observer however, is located in his space and time and observes strangely coupled events and paranormal facts in weirdly connected channels which he cannot fit into his normal logic and which are divorced from himself. He theorizes that events follow the pattern of dreams and tendencies while the fluid ego lives these processes. The dream world of the chronological observer is composed of separate localities, as static states with weird post-Einsteinian noncausal connections, while the fluid ego experiences only processes. The chronological observer is like the classical physicist. The fluid observer is a new type of psychologist-physicist who participates in the world he observes.

Still another type of observer can be discovered who is a mixture of the first two! A process scientist. He is able to both participate and hold his distance from events. He identifies himself with his primary processes in time and space, and also with the stream of events, those secondary perceptions. He maintains his normal sober intellectual consciousness while simultaneously participating in processes. He sees that all is his process but, because he is also in space and time, realizes the existence of static outer world order. For him, the world is a dream-world reality, a constantly changing mixture of real things and dream-like phenomena.

The dream world is a process which he describes in terms of channels, tendencies or chance occurrences according to his own reactions. He realizes the existence of stable states and process logic, but sees that they are momentary phases of a dream-world process. For him observing events and experiencing processes, thinking and feeling are all momentary states of his own evolving. His relationship to processes is fluid. He may be as analytical in one moment as he may be process oriented in another. He would correspond to a psychological ideal, the integrated or whole individual, someone who is simultaneously involved and clear about his involvement.

### UNIFYING PSYCHOLOGY AND PHYSICS

At present the average physicist and psychologist are chronological observers who participate only minimally in their observations. The physicist sits in time and space and wonders at the mysteriousness of a natural universe in which signals travel in unknown ways. The average psychologist either analyzes states or tries to program change. Their bondage to chronological reference frames creates as many theoretical problems as it solves.

The Newtonian concepts such as the conscious and the unconscious prove inapplicable, for example, to psychotic states, deep body experiences and parapsychological or out-of-the-body experiences, where the very idea of the ego is difficult to define. Likewise the concepts or channels called matter and psyche are too vague to be practical to enable us to work efficiently with psychosomatic problems. Jung would say that the sciences are still in the 'mother', in a state of potential which has not yet touched concrete reality.

There are several notable attempts in physics to change this situation around, and to redevelop theory more closely with the changing aspect of our world.[22] According to Finkelstein, 'classical quantum mechanics is a hybrid of classical concepts (space, time) and quantum concepts (states, tests). A more consistently quantum mechanics is proposed, with space, time and matter replaced by one primitive concept of process.'[23] Bohm, in his *Wholeness and the Implicate Order*, tells us that 'flow is, in some sense, prior to that of the "things" that can be seen to form and dissolve in this flow.' He has also said that 'various patterns that can be abstracted from it have a certain relative autonomy and stability, which is indeed provided for by the universal law of the flowing movement.'[24]

Psychologists and physicists have believed in process structures for centuries. But belief is not enough. Process science is a study of perception, and until we realize that the way we observe is strongly determined by our primary process identity of remaining cool, objective and whole, we shall lack the necessary awareness required to translate dreams of the 'new age' into reality. The changes implied by process science can not happen over night because they are based upon a highly refined awareness only dreamed about until now at least by Buddhists, Taoists and modern physicists.

It is difficult to know what sort of theory will develop to deal with psychotic, parapsychological and political events but it will have to explain the apparent consciousness of the field we live in and be more closely related to our experience of ourselves. Perhaps the world will turn out to be an anthropos figure after all, a mythological structure mirroring the nature of its perceiver, man himself.

In any case in a post-Einsteinian universe, where telepathy, synchronicity, dreams and somatic body trips occur, the concept of process unifies events which move from psyche to matter, imaginations into the body. This concept allows psychology and physics to come together and allows the process worker to deal with post-Einsteinian signals and channels, regardless of their inner mechanisms or superluminal nature.

According to process concepts we can look at any event such as synchronicity from the viewpoint of the individual or from the viewpoint of the collective, depending upon which dreamer or observer we are dealing with. Thus, for example, from the individual's point of view, the bear or god synchronicity were dreamed up in the environment in part to show the individual in a differentiated fashion, more about his own bear-like nature. A bear-like tendency or archetype, an implicate order or probabilistic pattern, was present in his personality trying to enfold and express itself.

From the viewpoint of the collective, the individual dreamer was part of a group process whose pattern dealt with the bear archetype or its amplifications in terms of the wild and ecstatic and berserker behavior found, for example, in early Germanic mythology. The individual dreamer was then part of the collective unconscious, he represented an aspect of the group process which was not yet in the foreground of common awareness. Therefore, this group witnessed his process. In this moment, he became a channel for the world just as it had been a channel for his process.

The process scientist sees the individual as a world unto himself or understands the universe as a unity with parts such as people and objects. These parts think they are independent beings and sometimes forget that they themselves are channels for a greater process happening right now.

# Part II
# THE ROOTS OF
# PROCESS CONCEPTS

# Chapter 6
# PROCESS MYTHOLOGY

Process concepts are becoming increasingly popular with advances in psychology and physics. However, like these sciences, process work itself is a process whose roots turn endlessly backward through alchemy, primitive religion, Taoism and mythology. Since tracing these roots gives us a fuller understanding of the implications of process concepts, I have chosen to devote the second part of this work to discussing the origins of process concepts found in the energy and time symbols appearing in mythology and religion.

Mythological and religious concepts appear cyclically like threads in historical patterns. Thus, early Greek analytical thinking is now being replaced by something like Taoistic thought in modern physics. The different forms of modern psychology also have religious patterns behind them. This fact explains why the followers of different schools are so fervently involved in their propagation. For example, something like wotanic and violent Yawehistic deities appear in modern gestalt practices which recommend 'losing the mind' in order to 'gain the senses.' There is definitely something light and fun-loving, something Dionysian, about humanistic psychology's stress upon the reduction of suffering and the enjoyment of life. The confessional, serious and abreactive aspects of classical psychoanalysis are vaguely reminiscent of a primitive's penitence after having broken a religious law or taboo set up by the gods. Process work, too, has something like theology in its background. It tends to be a nature religion, embracing all the divinities. Thus, in any given session, the unfolding of a given process is likely to encompass shy confessions, ecstatic explosions, berserk expression of fury or thoughtful analytical reflection. In the first part of this book I have chosen to discuss process in terms of its modern formulations by using concepts such as information, signals, channels, awareness, primary and secondary phenomena, dreambody events, relationships and physics. In the second part I wish to go back to the roots of process concepts found in mythology, Taoism and alchemy because these ancient traditions, rituals and beliefs contain the seeds of modern ideas. Discussion of these ancient process systems will give us more under- standing of where modern concepts come from and what they may be missing. Hopefully the study of mythology will lend us some objectivity upon the development and state of modern psychology and physics. Let us look at process ideas as if we were anthropologists!

Anthropologically speaking process science is that sort of tribal religion which believes in nature divinities. Other tribes place their gods above those of other peoples and create a hierarchical mythology and animosity towards the divinities of their neighbors. Process science, however, does not place one god over another, matter over psyche, body over mind, sex above power, the here and now over the past.

According to Joseph Cambell;

> In cultures dominated by nature deities you could go from one locality to another and say, 'The deity whom you call Neptune we call Poseidon, and so we have the same gods.' without getting into trouble.[1]

Western science, however, has tended to be hierarchical, until now at least. When Freud came across the archetype of sex, he expected others to feel that this was the most important god. Campbell points out that the Freudian ego tried to control the 'id' or instinct and thus mirrored Yahweh's animosity towards nature goddesses. Freud inadvertently created a sort of hierarchical theology which characterized western culture's fear of nature, of process. 'But nature,' Campbell argues, 'is not so chaotic. Energy comes to us already inflected, specified and organized . . .'[2] We would say process appears in exact channels with specific types of signals.

Jung's definition of psychic energy placed psychology in the realm of process science. Jung saw many gods in the psyche's pantheon, which he called the collective unconscious instead of sexual libido. Jung realized a nature mythology in which all gods were equal in the sense of sharing the same energy and potential significance for a given individual.

Einstein also relativized the gods Time, Space, and Matter. He realized that these latter divinities may transform into one another and called their basic stuff energy. Einstein implied in the general theory of relativity that matter, space and time are equivalent in the sense of transforming into numerical fields of energy. Thus, theoretical physics says essentially, 'the god you call matter we call energy and so we have the same god.'

Thus, even though our western tribe has had its prejudices, animosities and fears of process, this nature divinity has slipped into our sciences in the form of physic's energy and psychology's concept of the collective unconscious. Nevertheless our western fear of nature creates controls over process which must be kept under the domination of a sort of police force because, if it is not, we suspect process will create chaos. Einstein and Jung would agree with Campbell, however, and say that this fear or control is not quite justified for empirical nature appears to the observer in terms of inflected, quantized and organized energies, as quantum phenomena, numbers or, as I have pointed out in the preceding chapters, channels.

Since process is a nature divinity, it should not surprise us that it appears in terms of mythical time deities or that these figures carried with them divisions and organizations which quantized process in terms of channels!

**TIME**

Though the very idea of process is very very old, process consciousness will be a new form of thinking for many people because prevailing western consciousness is chronological and state oriented. Our consciousness and religious systems divide events up into predetermined categories such as life is good and bad, moral and immoral, healthy and sick.

However, we have not always possessed a polarizing, chronological consciousness which divides events into opposites. Christian thinking characterized by differentiated concepts such as good and evil was already beginning to wane in the medieval period. Von Franz points out that the seeds of change were sown in legendary figures such as Merlin the Magician who was good, evil and more.[3] He was mercurial, unpredictable and tricksterlike. Merlin prefigured the coming Aquarian age which is symbolized in astrology by the waterbearer who feeds the fish. Von Franz speculates that selfhood and individuation will become more important than the opposites in the coming perod of western consciousness.[4] If figures such as Merlin and the Aquarian waterbearer relativize the absoluteness of the opposites, then the Aquarian age might be typified by living with the flow of events in contrast to concepts about them, by the fluid not the chronological observer.

In order to imagine a process oriented consciousness we might look at our own early Greek psychology or at the mythology of modern non-technical peoples such as the American Indians. The Hopi Indians, for example, are process oriented. Their time concept does not include past or future but only that which 'is beginning to manifest' and 'that which is manifest', like rocks and objects.[5] We would call these 'secondary and primary processes!' They do not use future or past verb tenses but live close to phenomena themselves. For them the moment to do something is not predetermined, but an unpredictable creation requiring process awareness to know when 'something' is beginning to manifest. In contrast to the Hopi Indians a state-oriented consciousness watches the clock in order to know when to begin. The Hopi would in principle, watch events themselves.

I am neither predicting nor recommending that we transform our mentality into that of the Indians. We could not do so even if we wanted to because we are different from our less technical relatives. If a western, state-oriented individual becomes process oriented then part of his process is bound to be characterized by state-oriented thinking! In other words, he will be a total observer. There will be times when he follows his mental, divisive frameworks and other times when he allows his behavior to be governed by the flow of events themselves. There will be moments when he creates frameworks for existence and other moments when events create these frameworks.

From experience, I know that there are moments when it is easier to apply a given program to someone's process, and watch the results. When these programs make me uncomfortable or begin to block the client's growth and change I awaken and attempt to discover the structure of my client's process which is implicit in events. Only then do I look for primary and secondary phenomena, channels, double signals, etc. or ask the client to help me discover the structure in what is happening.

### OCEANOS

At the dawn of western history our concept of time was symbolized by the Greek figure of Oceanos.[6] Imagine him. He is pictured as an immense serpent encircling the world and sometimes carries the zodiac on his back. He has several interesting characteristics. First of all, his name shows us that he stands for water. He is god of the oceans. As a water demon he symbolizes flow and process. Early Greeks, like the Hopi Indians of today, were process or 'water' oriented.

Let us now consider Oceanos' serpent nature. Serpents, because of their undulating nature, point to the periodic nature of processes. Everyone who has studied himself over long periods of time will have noticed how typical problems and states are forever returning. One is periodically happy, then sad, free, then imprisoned, etc. In fact, processes are so periodic that we often predict that the opposite of the present state will soon occur even though we can not predict the speed or exact nature of the coming state. Thus serpents point to the periodicity of processes.

But serpents can be venomous too. The poisonous nature of processes occurs primarily when we are unconscious of them. Process work often shows us that criticism which has not been made conscious turns against us in the form of aggressive cramps. Dreams picture how an animal can become furious and bite us if we have neglected our instincts too long. The venomous aspects of processes often appears when one first begins to feel the way into dreams or body processes. A woman who refused to accept her fantasies, for example, was bitten in a dream by a bird (a fantasy symbol) which turned into a vicious snake.

2 *Double-headed serpent in turquoise mosaic, Mixtec workmanship, Mexico, 13th-14th century (British Museum)*

Ancient time concepts were process oriented and hence filled with unpredictable, lucky but also vicious powers. Such process concepts are vastly different from our modern mechanical idea of time. For example, in India, time is symbolized by the god Shiva or goddess Shakti or her sister Kali who represents the violent brutal nature of time.[7] Kali or a variation of her often appears in the processes of sick people who have been naive about their own reality. In their dreams, vicious ugly things often happen, prefiguring the catastrophic experiences which are awaiting them. Their processes have become deadly in part because they have not accepted the brutal aspects of their natures.

One of Oceanos' most interesting characteristics is that he is wrapped around the world. The snake wound around the world could picture human experience imprisoned by time. What does this mean? If we think in modern terms, then we

3  *Shiva with the River Ganges flowing from his head* (Crown copyright, *Victoria and Albert Museum*)

4 *Kali in her rage on the battlefield, overcoming Shiva, c. 1880 (Crown copyright, Victoria and Albert Museum)*

know right away what it means to be in a 'time cramp.' All of us at one time or another feel pressured to do things on time. We sometimes call this state of affairs a 'reality cramp.' It is partially caused by the way we organize life, preprogramming routines instead of letting things develop as they want to.

However, this interpretation of reality cramping is weak because the serpent is an unconscious animal, not a human being. To more fully understand our reality compulsion we have to consider the possibility that our processes are cramping us. Imagine for a moment that you are not part of the human world, but that instead you are a snake wound around the planet earth. Then you might have any one of a number of experiences. You might discover that you are cramping the world and yourself because you (as the world) are lazy and need a cramp in order to get something done. You might discover that you are cramping yourself because you need boundaries and homelife, security and warmth. You might be cramping yourself in order to discover your own strength. In any case, as soon as you identify with the reality cramp, you discover the snake and your own process. Immediately you experience your own psychophysical nature and withdraw your projections onto the surrounding world. 'Time' does not stress us, our own process wants to create boundaries, cramps, challenges, edges.

People who consciously experience their processes in dream body work with symptoms and projections frequently find themselves suddenly at the limits of reality. They are at their edge between primary and secondary processes. This experience is symbolized by Oceanos who forms the outer limits of the world, the boundary to the unknown. Process work brings one to one's edge, which may be described variously in such terms as 'far out,' disoriented, swimming, lost, 'spaced out' or 'not knowing where one is.' Oceanos is a process which rescues those who are insufficiently organized by creating structure and boundaries but disorients others who have been too controlling, too limiting. In other words, the way one approaches the edge determines Oceanos' behavior.

One way of approaching the edge of one's world is to refuse to admit that it is there and to go back to safe thinking and believing. Such a person is then usually flipped by Oceanos, the unwanted edge. I am thinking in the moment of a woman who entered a mental hospital saying that she was the great goddess Kali. I asked her why she wanted to cut off men's heads and she said because they were not nice to her. Apparently this woman could not face earlier realizations that her boyfriend did not like her. When he left her she flipped. Such an idea was an 'edge' for her and therefore flipped her identity. Another kind of person would have come to this information edge, and let the negative thoughts structure her changing relationship.

### THE KUNDALINI

One of the eastern equivalents of Oceanos who encircles the world would be the great serpent goddess Kundalini who is wound three and a half times around the base 'chakra' or center of the body, the 'muladhara,' the root or earth of the human being.[8] However there is an important difference between the Kundalini and Oceanos. He is wound around the world while 'she' is coiled up within the human body.

Thus while the western mind experiences stress mainly from outer world sources the Indian tends to be aware of imprisonment within the body. The Kundalini's winding about the base of the 'muladhara' is thus a symbol of body cramps, tensions, desires, armouring and potential energy.

The yogi in principle goes about releasing the Kundalini in a very different manner than a western therapist. The western body therapist tends to fight the cramps in the body trying to overcome them. Body symptoms for the yogi, however, are godlike, they are manifestations of Shakti or Kundalini which must, in principle, be worshipped, not repressed. The way of liberation in yoga is thus to meditate upon the Kundalini's windings, to focus breath and concentration on her until she spontaneously arises, shooting through the body and awakening it with streaming energy flow.

The yogi's method of liberation conforms to a process oriented psychology in which body phenomena are focused upon and amplified. Sometimes body processes ask for repression but most appear as the beginnings of new processes. The process oriented psychologist discovers that body problems can be the beginnings of an enlightening energy whose messages were somatized. In other words, the body is not necessarily full of pathological problems which must be overcome but of messages from coiled up or potential energy sources which must be tapped.

Consider a Kundalini experience I recently witnessed while working with an elderly man. He felt that there was a 'coil' in the center of his head, creating headaches. He amplified and meditated upon this coil by shaking his head to feel the pain more. Then he said, 'Oh, I want to be a coil and jump!' He moved his hands up and down, and so I recommended that he jump with his whole body. His immediate insight was, 'I have given up on life but I am actually still full of excitement and want to have more fun!' Here, a potential energy or process in his body was awakened, and led to an enlightening and insightful experience.

### AION

Before leaving the serpentine aspect of processes we must discuss Oceanos' later developments. Later Greeks conceived of him in terms of Chronos, Zeus and Aion.[9] Aion was a more complex development of Oceanos. Apparently Aion was originally a vital fluid in human beings which lived on after death of the individual in the form of a snake. Aion was also considered to be the creator and destroyer of all things and a sort of 'world soul.'[10] Aion was connected also to Mithras who appeared as a monster with a lion's head holding a staff around which a snake was coiled.[11] The signs of the Zodiac, Sol and Luna, together with the seasons also appear around this monster. Ogawa goes on to say that the snake was considered to represent the heavenly course of the seven planets while the staff was the tool or thunderbolt of the gods.

If we conceive of Aion as a development of Oceanos we can see how process concepts developed. Aion represents a more differentiated picture of processes than Oceanos. Aion includes subtle body or 'out-of-the body' experiences since

5  *Aion (Biblioteca Apostica Vaticana)*

he is a fluid transcending death. Aion's association to the universal course of the stars shows that individual processes also have collective and inorganic characteristics. Aion thus points to dreambody processes which transcend the life-death and personal-collective differentiations. Aion is a symbol of a world or universal consciousness, and thus of the collective unconscious, the universal dream field of which we are all parts.

In other words, our individual human process is not simply individual but has collective and universal aspects. This is why, when we identify ourselves at least partially with our processes, apparently personal difficulties and experiences frequently lead to cosmic feelings. Such feeling is considered enlightenment in many religions. The 'Kings' process discussed on page 59 of the last chapter is an example of such a cosmic experience. In her discussion of Ogawa's work, von Franz points out that Aion's lion nature symbolizes fiery spiritual power, while the snake corresponds to the monster's earthy, watery side.[12] She also points out that Aion as well as other supreme deities which are connected with time, such as the Dakota 'wakanda,' the Algonquin 'manitou,' the Australian Yao 'mulungu,' and the Melanesian 'mana,' are primitive energy concepts which are related to later Greek and modern quantitative concepts of energy. She traces the energy concepts into mathematical physics and also to Freud's libido and Jung's psychic energy.

Modern biologists relate energy to the concept of life as well. Asimov, for example, shows how the physicist's concept of energy (related to mechanical work) may be used as a measure for life and applied to the entire spectrum of inorganic and organic material events.[13]

Returning to Aion we notice first of all that two aspects of processes appear in him, the lion head and snake wound around the staff. The mythological amplifications indicate that the lion would represent the fiery spiritual aspect of processes, their tendency to manifest in dreams. The snake wound around the staff in the lion's hand implies that the original energetic dream impulses persevere in the sense of repeating themselves again and again. In other words, processes have dream-like beginnings which then periodically repeat themselves.

The differentiation of energy, time and process by Aion's

symbolism of dream impulses and perseverations bridges the gap between what we today define as body and mind. Modern energy concepts are less holistic. The physicists' definition of energy is quantitative, and measurable.

CONSERVATION PRINCIPLES

If we take a closer look at the sciences of psychology and physics we notice that the energy concept is really not as split as it looks at first sight. Physicists separate imagination from matter, enclose it in a box and notice that in a closed system measurable quantitative energy is neither created nor destroyed. This discovery, called the conservation of energy, also appeared to psychologists such as Jung, to fit psychic processes. In an article on psychic energy, he states that psychic energy tends to be conserved too.[14] When one is depressed, for example, energy flows out of consciousness into the unconscious, often into body symptoms. Energy never disappears but transforms and may reappear in dreams, inner or outer life. Or, in other words, energy or process is always present in one or more channels. If it is not in dreams or visualizations, it is often found proprio-ceptively. If it is neither in the dream nor in the body, it is found in relationship phenomena.

One way of putting psychology, biology and physics back together again is by leaving the modern energy concept for the moment and focusing on its archaic predecessor, Aion, i.e. process. One of the advantages of talking about processes instead of energies is that we are no longer bound by the latter's modern implications, its quantitative and qualitative definitions. Process is related to the occurrence of events and not to any one of their particular qualitative or quantitative characteristics. Process is a psycho-physical or neutral description of events and accords with symbols such as Oceanos and Aion who were simultaneously inner body experiences, outer organic life, universal and spiritual phenomena. The concept of process and information thus bridges modern terms such as matter, psyche, life and even energy.

## CONSERVATION AND TRANSFORMATION

One of the widespread beliefs found in world religions is life after death. If we formulate this belief in terms of process theory then we come upon a conservation pattern. Of course we do not know for certain whether processes are really conserved or whether people really go on existing after death. We can only take this motif as a speculation. But the speculation is so ancient and so persistent that we must also ask if there is not a natural law, a pattern or an archetype involved.

The analogous concept in modern science to the religious belief of life after death would be the conservation of energy in physics and psychology. The process description of the conservation of energy would be the idea that *process is constant*. Process may manifest or transform in different ways, but yet, it is a potential constant for a given observer. The belief of surviving death thus implies a natural law such as the conservation of process. Human observers are processes which transform but are basically conserved over time and space. Process awareness is then equivalent to the experience of immortality, liberation or freedom from time and death which the yogis call being dead in life.[15]

The evidence of the conservation of processes extending beyond death occurs frequently in dying people and has been discussed in the last chapter of my *Working With the Dreaming Body*. The conservation of processes is a different problem in the living, however. Here the question for the empirically oriented psychologist or process worker is not, does awareness go on after death, but where does information go now? The answer from the foregoing work is that process is constant and appears in one of the channels of perception. If it is not in dreams, it is in the body, the outside world or another person!

## ZODIACS AND CHANNELS

Channels appear in connection with process symbols such as the Kundalini, Oceanos and Aion. Oceanos and Aion were pictured with the zodiac. The Kundalini appeared with a chakra system. The zodiac was, in early Greek times, considered to be a map of the stars, a description of how the universe evolved. Each stage of its process corresponded to a particular constellation, and each constellation was described, like star groupings today, in terms of dramatic constellations. Thus the zodiac is a symbol of a process's possible channels or modes of manifestation.

Today time is no longer divided up into phases governed by the deities but is measured mechanically. Thus we scarcely realize the divine qualities behind our dimensions of reality. The divine nature of our channels appears whenever they are called into question. Then we realize they were parts of our personal theologies. Many people today, for example, still try to repress the existence of parapsychological phenomena and get emotional about inconsistencies in their dearly prized concepts of time and spaces. Body therapists feel body channels are all powerful, dreamers feel dreams are god. Physicists believe only in the measurable, psychologists think physicists are rationalists, etc.! Channels themselves are like gods corresponding to people's psychology and beliefs.

FRAMING

Oceanus did not flow into a prescribed maze set up for him. He carried the zodiac on his back! Since the zodiac is a symbol of process channels we can understand the zodiac being carried on the back as a picture of processes carrying their own channels.

If we try to organize events as if we were chronological observers then we frame processes before they occur. If we watch events themselves and see what sort of frameworks they carry with them (on their backs!) then we are no longer state-oriented 'framers' but process-oriented scientists.

Framing often mirrors people's worst problem: deciding what to do ahead of time, pressing themselves to do things whether or not they feel like it and regardless of the direction of events. Framing life instead of letting it determine its own process is, psychologically speaking, an inflation. One has inadvertently identified oneself with the governor of nature, the gods. Framing nature is so common that most of us do not notice a most dangerous inflation, in attempting to rule life.

Reference to other cultures is humbling and relativizing. One notices in the Aztec myths, for example, how the framework of reality is created by the process itself and not by human consciousness. In their creation myth the Aztecs imagine a god called Omtéotl, the original and supreme deity (like Aion) who was mother and father of all.[16] They tell us that he was 'a mirror that illumines all things.'

In our terms, this god would be the process, the creator of existence who illuminates by mirroring. Everyone knows this mirroring in the phenomena of perseverating, doubling and repeating. We become conscious of our process because it constantly repeats itself, dreaming up the world around us reflecting until we see what is happening. If we do not see it, the process continues to repeat, it goes into a cycling activity which we experience as feeling 'stuck' or going around in circles.

CREATING CHANNELS

However, I am not telling the Aztec myth in order to reflect upon process but upon the channels it creates. The myth continues and tells us that Omtéotl created four more gods, the so-called Tezcatlipocas, who in turn created the world. These four gods were identified with the directions of the compass with specific animals and colors. These directions, animals and colors symbolize the channels in which human processes of growth can manifest themselves and are the dimensions of Aztec reality.

If we translate this myth into process terms then we see that the process itself, Omtéotl, the mother and the father of all things, also creates its own dimensions. This myth compensates 'common sense.' We tend to think that if we do not structure nature that it will create chaos. We feel that *we* are responsible for holding nature together. If we do not plan and define everything in advance the world is going to fall apart. Naturally there are moments when it is important to use ordinary consciousness and to define what is going to happen and to hold to this program. But frequently the opposite is true.

RELATIVITY AND CHANNEL SYSTEMS

The Aztec myth tells us that Omtéotl creates the gods, that processes manifest new and unpredictable channels. Thus, sticking to one set of channels can be unnecessarily limiting to growth and change.

Let me give an example from India. Myths tell us, for example, that the Kundalini created the world and then settled down in the base of the 'muladhara' to rest.[17] Part of the world she created was the chakra system, the seven body 'channels' located in specific parts in the body. Routinely using only this system can be inhibiting to body work, however, because each person's process develops their body channels in specific and not altogether predictable ways. Thus body centers may appear in places which do not correspond to the Indian chakra system. *Any place* a symptom manifests itself is a potential channel for processes to occur! Thus the chakra system is only one possible frequently occurring system of channels but not the only one.

Jung's discovery of dream imagery he called the anima, animus, shadow and self would correspond to the Indian chakra system insofar as these dream figures are centers or channels through which the unconscious manifests itself in imagery. An uncreative dream worker will not pick up the individual dream language but frame dreams in this known system just as an uncreative body therapist works according to given programs instead of the phenomena themselves.

STOPPING THE WORLD

A chronological observer who frames processes into states instead of letting them create their own dimensions, dreams up life to become unpredictable and worn out. Frequently fate impinges from outside upon such a person from dreams, body problems, relationships and accidents threatening to upset or even stop the world one is living in. Castaneda's shaman-tutor Don Juan would say that such fate is a moment when one should 'stop the world.' He should consciously follow the disturbances and stop perceiving reality in the old channels, let new modes of awareness arise.

Naturally, one cannot change channels simply because one chooses to do so. Real change happens when the world is stopped as processes themselves recreate channels. When such changes take place, the world as we experience it, together with some of our gods and belief systems, loses its former validity. The loss of these systems always coincides with temporary feelings of disorientation. Xenophobia, fear of new and unexperienced life occurs together with death of the old gods and confrontation with the ineluctable flow of nature, the Tao. This fear frequently maintains the old channels, while threats of destruction impinge from the universe.

According to the newspapers, the threat of nuclear war can be understood as one unconscious and unnecessary way of stopping the world. The alternative to this negative and destructive aspect of Oceanos, Omtéotl, Aion and Kali would be a transformation in the way we perceive and process the world. Either we participate in channel changes and relativize our control over events, or we will become overly fascinated with really stopping the world. The violence of ancient process gods is a warning to us as individuals and nations to restructure life as much as possible from day to day instead of from lifetime to lifetime.

# Chapter 7
# CHANNELS IN TAOISM

Process science appears spontaneously wherever people follow the flow of events as distinct from preconceived notions about how they should go. I pointed out in the last chapter that process and channel concepts are not really new ideas, but are found in old Greek and Aztec Indian time theories, in ancient myths.

The most complete process theory which I have come across until now is expressed in the main oracles of Taoism, the *Tao Te Ching* and the *I Ching*. I show in this chapter how these ancient texts offer us a philosophical and numerical basis for developing process theory.

I strongly recommend to the reader who is unfamiliar with Taoism to study the *Tao Te Ching* and experiment with the *I Ching* if he wants to know more about process work. Introducing these texts here in a complete way is beyond my resources. Their philosophy is difficult to translate and their methods of ascertaining the Tao must be experienced. I can only hint here at the phenomenological psychology I feel lies hidden in their messages.

The Taoists were first-class process scientists. They observed events, noted their spontaneous arrangements and did not doubt or attempt to explain them. I would call them religious scientists but the term 'religious' is misleading because they had no special gods. In fact our pantheon of deities finds no analogy in Taoism. There the single and most important principle is simply process, that is, following the Tao.

**THE TAOIST AS PROCESS WORKER**

In fact, *Tao Te Ching* and *I Ching* can almost be directly translated to mean process science. According to Raymond van Over, Tao is usually taken to mean the way or the path along which all things move.[1] Te refers to activity in the world. Thus Tao Te would mean, 'the way of activity' which is very similar to one of the Oxford Dictionary's definitions of process as the 'course of action'. Richard Wilhelm reports in his *Eight Lectures on the I Ching*, that 'I' means changes as shown, for example, in the symbol of a salamander or snake which changes its skin periodically. 'Ching' refers to a text or pattern as one finds in weaving and cloth. Hence, 'I Ching' means process as perceived in terms of the changes occurring in given patterns.

Let us focus for the moment on the Chinese word for the Tao itself. The word for Tao was originally derived from the same root as the words for sage, king and priest.[2] Priest and king then connoted the maximum human achievements, divining, communicating and following natural forces. Thus, the word Tao implies following nature as a guide.

The root word connecting priest, Tao and sage was composed of three horizontal lines standing for heaven, earth and man. This trigram was connected by a vertical line which completed the word for Tao. ( 三 ) Heaven, earth and man were designations for the way in which nature manifests itself. That is they are channels roughly equivalent to what we call psychic stuff or dreams, conscious situations and material events such as body problems. Using process language we can say that the Tao is the flow of events in and between channels. Tao signifies a process which simultaneously manifests in a number of different channels. Since the word for sage has the same root as Tao, a sage would be a process worker; a person who congruently mirrors processes manifesting in dreams, body and environmental phenomena.

Helmut Wilhelm warns us:

It is in constant change and growth that life can be grasped. . . . If it is interrupted, the result is not death, which is really only an aspect of life, but life's reversal, its perversion. . . . The opposite of change in Chinese thought is growth of what ought to decrease, the downfall of what ought to rule.[3]

If the Tao ought to rule, then the opposite to the Tao would be a tyrant, a 'framer' who insists on determining how things should go. The opposite to the sage or the Tao is an 'anti-process,' a state-oriented attitude which preprograms behavior and frames events before they occur. Thus the opposite to process is a predetermined standardization, a therapy, rule or goal.

## TAO AND WHOLENESS

According to Granet, the concept of Tao underwent many changes in the evolution of Chinese thought. Early Taoists saw the Tao as a mysterious and unfathomable process. Later Taoists, however, understood the Tao as a static balance between opposites such as yin and yang and pictured this balance in the famous yin-yang symbol.

According to the *I Ching* the yin-yang symbol was originally meant to represent the 'primal beginning' as including the two polar forces of the universe. Tao, an invisible way, serves to maintain the interplay of these forces so that they are constantly regenerated, constantly in tension, a constant potential creating the world anew in every moment, but without ever becoming manifest. There is always a state of tension between these primal powers, which keeps the 'world' constantly regenerating itself. In process terms there is always a state of tension between primary processes of which we are aware and secondary ones of which we are less aware. This state of tension is maintained by the edge. The total world or Tao thus rarely manifests because, as our awareness grows, the edge which separates processes continually moves just one step beyond our reach, and we must create new awareness and channels to reach it. Thus the yin-yang symbol did not originally represent a static concept, but rather a renewal of tension.

This later and more static concept of the Tao sharply contrasts its earlier conception. The earlier Tao is a process which creates the world and its channels. The later static concept of the Tao mirrors present state-oriented psychological concepts of human totality. These concepts picture wholeness as a balance of already existing opposites such as good and bad.

This state of 'wholeness' then becomes a fixed goal in most cases which the growing person much achieve through effort. He tries to mechanically create balances and harmonies within himself. Theoretically such a person could not suffer from strong emotional conflicts.

The earlier concept of the Tao, however, implies that a sage or an individuated person is one who is aware of processes and who adjusts himself according to this awareness. He does not attempt to create balance with his will but instead tries to know and then follow what is happening.

The state-oriented person perceives such a 'sage' as unpredictable. It is unlikely that the process-oriented Taoist would debate later Taoist ideas. However, if he did he might argue that organization and wisdom must be continuously discovered anew in the flow of events themselves.

## THE EVOLUTION OF PROCESS CONCEPTS

Apparently the early idea of the Tao as a creative flow lies behind Taoism's main oracles, the *Tao Te Ching* and the *I Ching*. Lao Tsu says in the former: 'The Tao which can be expressed in words is not the Tao.'[4] He is saying that our descriptions of events in terms of predetermined ideas and vocabulary does not accord with the reality of events themselves. I see the practicality of Lao Tsu's viewpoint in process work. There I observe how process students tend to use their preconceived systems of understanding in explaining the body processes of their student colleagues in supervision seminars. The student observer uses *his* channels to frame processes and not the spontaneous vocabulary and actions of events themselves.

Lao Tsu is suggesting that a 'beginner's mind'[5] is necessary in understanding the Tao. One has to keep one's perception open and see things as they are. However, if we examine the evolution of Taoism, we see that Lao Tsu's recommendation was not followed!

This evolution can be expressed approximately as follows. At first some scientist with a beginner's mind sees reality as it is and describes some of the channels it spontaneously produces. Students of this 'beginner's mind' then standardize the channels he saw and ignore the Tao which 'cannot be expressed with words.' As time passes events occur which no longer conform to the logic of the older channels and someone with a 'beginner's mind' appears again and rediscovers Lao Tsu's Taoism.

And so it goes. First there is a unitarian theory of nature accompanied by a fresh description of life in terms of new channels of growth. This description is dogmatized and soon becomes inappropriate as events overlap old channels, relativizing their absoluteness. These events create or recreate holistic theories which relegate the significance of channels to second-order principles with respect to process.

Many examples of such an evolution will come to the reader's mind. Every change of religious order is a manifestation of changing channels. The Jewish god Yahweh could be heard but not visualized. Jesus could also be seen! Physics and psychology are channels which replaced the earlier concepts of alchemy. Time and space were overcome by relativistic events. Divisibility and causality have been seriously shaken by quantum physics. Psychosomatic phenomena and parapsychological events are loosening the rigid border still separating psychics from psychology. As psyche and matter flow together, physiological categories such as the five senses will disappear and new descriptions of matter will arise out of the inapplicability of the old ones.

### AMPLIFICATION

If process science is itself a process then how can we catch it long enough to formulate it? Fortunately, people have been asking themselves this question for at least four thousand years in China and have summed up their conclusions in what we now know as the *I Ching*. Here we find an unprecedented integration of centuries of thought about the mysterious Tao and its channel creations. For example the *I Ching* explains the Tao as that: 'which completes the primal images (and) is called the creative. (The Tao) which imitates them is called the receptive.'[6] Here process is divided into 'creative' and 'receptive.' According to the *I Ching*, the creative phase of processes energizes or creates the 'primal images,' the channels. The receptive phase of a process 'imitates' or repeats the original impulses in the channels.

The *I Ching's* Tao reminds us of the Aztec deity Omtéotl who created the four channel gods, the Tezcatlipocas, who in turn imitated their creater by then creating the world. Omtéotl was the 'creative' while Tezcatlipocas would be the 'receptive.' Aion, the Greek process god, also had a creative phase or lion phase and a repetitive phase symbolized by the coiled snake on his staff.[7]

The *I Ching's* ancient saying has practical consequences for process work. The text tells us that processes manifest themselves energetically by creating specific channels, the so-called primal images. Processes repeat or perseverate in these channels in the receptive phase.

If process work follows the Tao, then its first job is to recognize energetic manifestations in terms of channels, and to accurately observe their perseverations. Examples illustrate amplification.

If a patient resists a certain therapy process or has a negative projection upon the therapist, then amplifying resistance might mean encouraging the client to consciously assist his aggressiveness.

If someone sees powerful visions and searches for their meaning, then the search for meaning requires amplification through mythology, fairy tales or personal associations. If someone is fascinated by the colors and figures of a dream, then the colors may be amplified by visual (imaginary) intensification. The figures may be talked to or acted out. If someone cannot stop scratching his skin, the itch might be mechanically amplified in order to see what it wants. If there is pain in the stomach, then a proprioceptive message asks for conscious reception. In any case, the specific methods of amplification are derived exactly from processes themselves. The novice student of process work generally faces two basic problems. Firstly, he may feel responsible for something happening and feel he should play creator. Then he 'pushes', that is he tries to recommend new ideas and therapies so that processes will occur. Or, he becomes impatient when things finally do happen and does not give them a chance to persevere. If he ignores perseverations he will not learn from events themselves what and how to amplify. In this case he compensates for insufficient observation and lack of patience by applying standard procedures which are not tailored to the individual situation. Then his work becomes erratic and exhausting. In either case the student therapist suffers from feeling too important.

### ANALYZING AND EXPERIENCING
The *I Ching* continues to explain process science to us by further differentiating the Tao: 'In that it (the Tao) serves for exploring number and knowing the future, it is regulation. In that it makes for organic coherence in change, this is the work.'[8] Here we find a description of how the *I Ching* works. The Tao unfolds itself in the hexagrams through expressing itself in terms of the binary system, the yin-yang code, and a combination of this code, in six different channels (e.g. ☰☰ ). Insofar as events manifest themselves spontaneously in images such as binary codes, hexagrams, or in terms of dream pictures, acoustical tones, pains and proprioceptive sensations, the Tao creates and lets us 'explore' patterns or 'numbers.'

These patterns in turn give us 'regulation.' In other words, we can see the overall map of what has happened and what is likely to occur next by examining the hexagrams, dreams, body phenomena, etc. 'Knowing the future' and 'exploring number' are basic process analysis activities. We examine processes and try to understand their implicit patterns.

However, the very same Tao which unfolds the images, associations and representations also creates 'organic coherence in change.' According to the *I Ching* this 'organic coherence' is 'the work.' The *I Ching* thus defines process work in terms of analytically 'exploring number' or the patterns behind things and then experimentally following processes organically.

'The work,' like the alchemist's 'opus,' is transformation. No amount of knowledge can replace the experiential aspect of the Tao because without involvement in the evolution of visions, noises, body sensations, extrasensory perceptions, transference phenomena, or synchronicities, processes remain empty patterns without life.

The value of experiencing cannot be overestimated, especially since psychologists early in this century placed much importance upon insight and understanding as a cure for all things. The one-sided aspect of insight was naturally soon compensated for by another one-sidedness, experiencing. The existentialists in contrast to the psychoanalysts tend to see events as they are and require experiencing without critical analysis. Taoism or its modern correlate, process work, combine analyzing and experiencing according to the *I Ching*. In one phase of a given person's process exploring number or analyzing is the Tao while in another time experiencing the unpredictable flow of things is the Tao. Analysis and experience do not conflict, each has its own time.

**PROCESS UNCERTAINTY PRINCIPLE**

The *I Ching* continues its discussion: 'That aspect (of the Tao) which can not be fathomed in terms of the light and dark is called the spirit.'[9] In order to define this 'spirit' we must find out just how much of the Tao or of processes can actually be fathomed by the process in these channels. I can guess in which channels new experiences will occur but I cannot tell exactly what form the new experiences are going to have or when they will happen. Only process can reveal this information. For example, a woman who suffers from stomach trouble experiences her stomach as full of feeling. She dreams that a feelingless man dies. Her situation implies that she is moving out of feelinglessness and into the world of emotions and feelings, into stomach and gut reactions, into body or proprioceptive sensations. However I cannot tell her exactly *what* feelings are going to arise nor can I tell her *when* these are going to take place. Only living will reveal this.

The maximum amount of information which we can give someone about their process involves the channel in which they are functioning, the probable new channels which may open up, and the patterns of their present behavior in terms of primary and secondary phenomena. Jung formulated some of this information in terms of opposites. He discovered years ago that dreams are compensations for conscious behavior.[10] In process terms we would say that the secondary moves in a direction which is likely to be the opposite of momentary behavior. If one identifies with being weak we can guess that they will eventually become stronger and that their secondary processes are full of power signals. If they are having trouble in one channel such as seeing, or if they are plagued by a negative father who is determining and programming reality, we can guess that they are going to move into an unprogrammed life-style and let their eyes focus freely and randomly.

That which cannot be fathomed in terms of light and dark, in terms of the channels or their opposites is, according to the *I Ching*, the 'spirit.' In terms of the above, the 'spirit' is the unfathomable aspect of process work. It is the speed and exact form of future processes, the moment when channel changes occur, or when total awareness of the Tao will happen.

Thus processes contain an uncertainty principle which implies that their predictability is limited. We cannot guess when or exactly how things will manifest.

## ARCHETYPES IN THE I CHING

Jung's definition of the archetypes sounds very much like process structures or hexagrams.[11] According to Jung,

> archetypes are not determined as regards their content, but only as regards their form, and even then to a very limited degree. . . . Its form, however, might perhaps be compared to the axial system of a crystal, which performs the crystaline structure in the mother liquid although it has no material existence of its own. The first appears according to the specific way in which the ions and molecules aggregate. The archetype in itself is empty and purely formal, nothing but a possibility of representation which is given a priori. . . our comparison with the crystal is illuminating in as much as the axial system determines only the stereometric structure but not the concrete form of the individual crystal. This may be either large or small, and it may vary endlessly by reason of the different size of its planes or by the growing together of two crystals. The only thing that remains constant is the axial system, or rather the invariable geometric proportions underlying it. . .[12]

Jung's definition of the archetypes describes them as process structures with a common mathematical basis. Certain aspects of this basis, such as Jung's 'axial systems', refer to the dimensions of the archetypes, or the channels of their expression. The tendency of one archetype to run into another (the tree may be related to the sun which is connected to the father, etc.[13]) is explainable by reference to this common structure.

It is not the least bit surprising that other process-oriented systems such as the *I Ching* have very similar concepts to the archetypes. In what follows, I am going to relate the archetypes to the hexagrams, and attempt to derive aspects of the former from the latter. According to the *I Ching* itself, these hexagrams were constructed originally as follows:

> The holy sages determined the Tao of heaven and called it dark and light. They determined the Tao of the earth and called it the yielding and the firm. They determined the Tao

of man and called it love and rectitude. They combined these
fundamental powers and doubled them. . .[14]

and in this way developed the hexagrams. Those who are
familiar with the *I Ching* will recognize in this ancient
formulation not only a description of the archetypes but a
description of how the oracle is used. The diviner first
formulates and contemplates a basic question in as simple a
manner as possible. When he is clear about this question
and has achieved an open mind to the ways of fate through
the use of incense or meditation he then enters into a ritual
procedure in which he allows fate to unfold itself.[15]

The *I Ching* employs one of two numerical rituals for this
procedure. One is called the yarrow stalk method in which
the questioner randomly divides forty-nine yarrow stalks
and computes the result so that one of two outcomes must
occur, yin or yang represented respectively by a divided
line, a ———— , or – –. The second method is a coin-throw
procedure in which three coins are flipped. Their outcomes
again are calculated in terms of the same binary system. The
result of repeating any one of the two procedures, (that is
the yarrow stalk or the coin throw) six times is the so-called
hexagram, a picture with six lines such as ═══⊖═══ The
possible sixty-four permutations and combinations of these
six lines have particular names and are described and
commented on by the *I Ching*.

A psychological commentary on the *I Ching*'s hexagrams
would be a work unto itself, and certainly worth perform-
ing. Here, however, I am going to examine only the
numerical properties of the hexagrams.

### THE CHANCE ASPECT OF ARCHETYPAL IMAGES

One of the most fundamental properties of the hexagrams is
their chance-like nature. The hexagrams are created in such
a way as to cancel out ego manipulation. The questioner is
requested from the beginning to empty his mind of any
desire for a particular outcome. Then he enters into a
procedure which he cannot influence in any known causal

way. In the coin throw, for example, he is not able to influence the movement of the coins unless we speculate some form of magical or parapsychological causality. Such speculative theories are basically foreign to the *I Ching* which merely assumes that a chance event is a measure of the Tao. If we translate the chance aspect of the hexagrams into practical process work, then we arrive at a useful consideration. Namely, the archetype appears spontaneously in a multitude of channels through non-ego action.

ARCHETYPES AND CHANNELS
The archetype is the connecting pattern organizing spontaneous events. Thus dreams would be a channel of the archetype since one has minimal control over them. Body problems which cannot be influenced in a causal manner would be another channel of the archetype. Spontaneous acts of fate also belong to the description of the archetype. We see that the archetype is a total picture of the spontaneous phenomena occurring in all possible channels.

Notice that the hexagrams are a composition of *six* lines, or (according to the *I Ching* itself) a doubling of three lines. What are these three lines? The ancient sages determined the Tao of heaven, earth and man and then doubled these Taos, thereby creating the hexagrams.

What is the meaning of heaven, earth and man? The reader will recall from the previous chapter that the manner in which processes appear was discussed in terms of their individual characteristics or channel modes of communication. Heaven, man and earth would thus correspond to the channels in which the old Chinese experienced the workings of processes.

A careful reading of the *I Ching* might allow us to approximately translate heaven, man and earth in terms of what we today consider to be the world of dreams (heaven), the world of ordinary life (man), and the realm of inorganic and organic existence such as the body (earth). I cannot give an exact translation of the Chinese channels in terms of ours because their concepts overlap our modern ones and make a one-to-one correspondence impossible. My translation merely emphasizes the idea that the Tao expresses itself in terms of channels.

The *I Ching*'s use of three basic channels seems to be more a description of the human being's message-receiving capacity rather than an absolute quality of nature itself. The reader will recall, for example, that when Omtéotl created the world, he first created four Tezcatlipocas who were the dimensions or channels of reality. The *I Ching* uses three such channels, the fourth is the movement or change implicit in the three. Modern people still tend to organize nature in terms of the three spatial coordinates and one of time which is the movement implicit within the three, or in terms of space and three time dimensions (past, present and future).

Modern psychology too has channel-like dimensions. Freud's channel to the unconscious, which he called the 'royal road,' was dreams. The existentialists say that the 'here and now', the foreground or behavior of things, is everything, the 'royal road,' so to speak. Wilhelm Reich and his followers used the body as another 'royal road.' So today, we understand the human personality to be a (not yet unified) combination of dreams, here and now consciousness, and body life.

In any case, a practical consideration arises from the manifold channel composition of hexagrams. Namely, an archetype is a doubling or repetitive pattern appearing spontaneously in three or four relatively independent channels.

Hence, a total picture or hexagram, an archetype or pattern of a given situation is one which includes repetitive body problems, dreams, here and now pictures or other individual channels which process work evolves. The process definition of an archetype is the interrelationship between various channels.

### BINARY CHARACTERISTICS OF ARCHETYPES

An important aspect of the hexagrams is that they are composed of binary information: yin and yang, or 0 and 1. The reasons for using a binary system are not discussed by the ancient sages. For them, things are simply the way they are and that is that. I accept the fact that the binary code is a basic method of communication between the non-ego and the ego, however, and I would also like to share my ideas about this binary code.

My theory about the binary code is based upon our innate ability to perceive things. Human beings are special types of receivers. Either we notice something or we do not. We are stimulated and pick up information, or we are not stimulated and perceive nothing. My theory does not involve the quality of information or its implicit message or meaning, but simply the process of our perception. The hexagrams are based upon the binary system of our reception apparatus, not upon the 'absolute' nature of the unconscious. The individual lines or channels are filled with binary signals yin or yang, without particular meaning attached to them! The significance of the binary code of any given channel appears only in terms of the total hexagram.

In process work, the binary system appears as the most primitive way a verbally oriented consciousness communicates with a non-verbal source of information. Let me give you an example. Let us say that you have a pain in your stomach. The most primitive communication between you and your stomach consists basically of a signal such as 'yes,' there is pain or 'no,' there is no pain. You could, if you wanted to, verbally communicate with your stomach without disturbing the authenticity of its proprioceptive communication potential by employing this system. For example, you could do a verbal proprioceptively oriented active imagination with your stomach if you determine for example that increased stomach pain means 'no,' decreased means 'yes.' Then you could ask the stomach anything you wanted to and get a yes or no answer. For example you might ask, 'Will you speak with me?' If pain increases (meaning 'no') you are too aggressive, passive, etc.

Let us say that a visual channel sends you a signal. A primitive verbal communication with the visual process asks it binary questions. You might say, 'Well, will you talk to me?' Increased intensity of light means 'yes,' etc. We should credit the neurolinguistic programmers for developing binary communication with auditory, visual and proprioceptive channels.

## BINARY FLICKERING

However, credit must be given to the *I Ching* for having developed binary communication with extrasensory sources. In fact the binary system of the *I Ching* is more differentiated than a simple 'yes-no' code. Studying this differentation leads to an extension of the simple binary system which then appears to be a special case of a more general method of communicating with the unconscious.

The *I Ching* manifests process in terms of a 'yes' and 'no' but also two other possible signals, thus enabling the non-verbal source to answer in a total of four signals: namely, yin, yin moving, yang and yang moving, corresponding to the numbers 6, 8, 7, and $9^{16}$ (and the results of throwing three coins whose 'heads' are valued three and 'tails,' two).

The 'moving' lines have extreme values (6 and 9) and are referred to as being especially 'charged.' These lines are used by the questioner to determine which line (or channel) of the overall hexagram (or archetype) is most applicable to his question. Change occurs in the overall hexagram because of these extremes or moving lines. If for example one gets a 9 in the fifth place and a 6 in the third in the following hexagram $\overset{\phantom{x}}{\underset{\phantom{x}}{\equiv}}$ (as well as a 7 in the first place, a 7 in the second, a 7 in the fourth and an 8 in the sixth) then only the 6 and 9 lines change. These lines change to their opposites thereby transforming the entire hexagram. Thus we have,

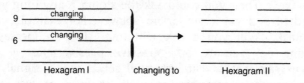

| 9 | changing | } | | |
| 6 | changing | → | | |
| | Hexagram I | changing to | Hexagram II | |

## An example

This representation of change in the archetypes gives rise to

special methods of communication with secondary processes. An example comes to mind. Imagine a man with a
stomach tumor. He is a simple man without particular
psychological interests and comes to me because he is afraid
of his tumor. He has no background in any of the
techniques of modern psychology which would help him to
contact his unconscious. He speaks about a pain in his
stomach and only about this pain. Amplifying and following
his process thus means staying in a verbally described
proprioceptive channel. He says, 'Sometimes the pain is
there and sometimes it is not. Why does it hurt me?' His
communication system is thus basically binary. 'What
question would you like to ask your stomach?' I say to him.
He repeats, 'Why do you hurt me so much?' Then I say, 'Try
to ask it something simpler which it can answer in yes and
no.' 'Will you tell me why you hurt me?' he asks. He focuses
on the pain which disappears and this means yes to him.
'Do you not like me?' The pain goes away again implying,
yes, it does not like him. 'Do you want to kill me?' Again a
yes. 'Will you tell me why?' Again a yes. 'Why?'

This time the pain goes away but flickers back again
indicating a yes but basically no. The secondary process says
it will tell him but that it does not want to. The flickering
answer indicates among other things that the unconscious
has an evolving and not a static answer. In other words the
answer is more than a simple 'yes' or 'no.' At this point the
receiver has one of two choices. He can reformulate his
question implicit in the flickering 'yes moving to no.'
Following the latter would mean momentarily dropping his
verbal framework and realizing that the unconscious is
speaking in terms of a proprioceptive process in contrast to a
static answer. Staying with a verbal receiver system limits
the expressiveness of the unconscious. If the receiver
chooses to examine this expressiveness then he must focus
his attention on proprioceptive channels and 'feel' with his
inner receptors and follow the pain's evolution. Such
following may require experience and practice.

In the present case, the man let his inner feeling evolve at
its own pace. After a while he 'felt' something and said that

his basic problem was that he had never had a relationship to himself. Then he felt better. Thus the answer to his question, 'why do you hurt me so much?' and also the solution to his pain occurred simultaneously.

The advantage of a simple binary system of communication is that it allows non-verbal sources to communicate in a verbal language framework without disturbing consciousness and without seriously perturbing the authenticity of the non-verbal source. Such a system can be especially useful to people who are novices in process work.

On the other hand the disadvantage of this system is that it limits a non-verbal source to a restricted communication potential. The 'moving lines' of the *I Ching* which correspond to binary flickering phenomena in a particular channel thus extend the static binary system. A binary flicker indicates the existence of a process. Following this process coming from a flickering channel or moving line, however, depends to some extent upon the individual's ability to temporarily abandon his normal communication framework and to enter another type of communication. This latter type may be experienced as a scary adventure. The choice about entering into this new communication can be determined only by the ego. If the fear is great, the fear is a process indicating that one must remain in one's own framework and press the unconscious to express itself there. A more adventurous situation would be indicated by less fear. Let us look at such a situation.

*Another example*
A man with a neck tumor complains about the fear and pain of the symptoms and repeatedly puts his hand on his neck. The flickering signal in the foreground which I shall amplify will be proprioceptive sensations in the neck. The dreams (visual channel) and relationship problems (relationship channel) may interest me but the proprioceptive experience in the neck is emphasized by the patient. The overall situation may be described by the case of an elderly man who has never been able to stand up for himself as a professional. He often suffers from inferiority feelings and

tends to be placating to others.

In this example amplification consists in introvertedly experiencing the tumor. After a few quiet moments the client says to me that he experienced his neck as if it were being strangled. Since he showed me with his hand what it was like to be strangled, I followed his motion and asked him to use that hand to strangle himself with. The 'strangler' promptly said, 'I shall kill you, you weak fish.' After more dialogue associated to the strangling activity, the neck muscles finally resisted saying that 'No one, not even fate is going to kill me.' This statement brought about an overall change in the man. He said that he was stronger than he had been aware of and that he now had to live his life without wondering 'how' to be strong but by simply 'being' strong. He said he felt better.

A process analysis of change based upon the numerical patterns of the *I Ching* would go something like this. The archetype or overall situation consists of an elderly man suffering from inferiority problems with one channel manifesting extreme flickering phenomena in the neck. The work focused on the neck and amplified the proprioceptive sensations there. The neck was the battleground between the weak and the strong. By amplifying the foreground experience of the strangler, the weak changed from weak to strong through the challenge. As soon as change happened in one channel an overall transformation occurred in which the neck felt better (there was a temporary relief from coughing caused by the tumor), insight into the personality spontaneously occurs and a program for future change was created.

Only the beginning and end phase of the processes can be described clearly. Amplification of the channel manifesting intense proprioceptive activity in the foreground, however, produced a moment in which there was no clarity, no governing picture or archetypal image. In terms used by the *I Ching* that aspect of the work which can be 'fathomed' in terms of the dark and the light (i.e. the opposites) would be the hexagram, i.e. the archetypal patterns of the beginning and end states. That aspect of the work which is 'unfathomable' in terms of the opposites (or their channels) is the 'spirit,' i.e. the speed and moment of change. In short the 'work' consists in letting the 'spirit' create 'organic coherence in change.'

The similarity in structure between the archetypes and hexagrams, lines and channels, moving lines and foreground channels, Tao and process are so striking that it seems certain that the same motivation which created the *I Ching* is trying to regenerate itself in modern times. This might be why the *I Ching* seemed to be ready to appear to western audiences.[17]

# Chapter 8
# PATTERNS IN THE I CHING

Now we move to a study of the hexagram or archetypal image as a whole and leave the investigation of its parts. The archetype is apparently more than the sum of its parts. It is the implication derived from individual channel characteristics.

According to Wilhelm,

> The situation represented by the hexagrams as a whole is called the Time. This term comprises several entirely different meanings according to the characteristics of the various hexagrams.[1]

The Time is further delineated by a very old Chinese mantic procedure in which a wheel with one set of trigrams is spun relative to another stationary wheel with another set of trigrams.[2] The resulting combination of the so-called earlier and later heaven arrangements is thus a combination of two times, an earlier and a later, or inner and outer, dream and reality. According to the *I Ching* the earlier heaven is composed of opposing forces which do not combat one another but rather hold each other in equilibrium. The later

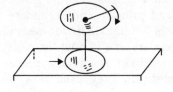

heaven is constructed according to the periodic changes in the day or the year. This later heaven arrangement comes out of the Lo River according to legend.

The view of the archetype as Time means that the archetype itself is a process, not a stationary condition. Helmut Wilhelm stresses process in his introduction to the *I Ching*:

> The eight trigrams are images not so much of objects as of states of change. This view is associated with the concept expressed in the teachings of Lao-Tse, as also in those of Confucius, that every event in the visible world is the effect of an 'image,' that is, of an idea in the unseen world.[3]

Wilhelm significantly reminds us that the hexagrams are not objects but processes, not static states but active in motion. The archetype is not the static momentary dream image or body problem but the 'process maker' so to speak, the repetitive impulse which amplifies itself in all channels of awareness.

### THE ARCHETYPE AS A DOUBLE PROCESS

If we return for a moment to the quote on page 99 of the foregoing chapter we recall that the sages created the hexagrams by determining the Tao in three channels and then doubling the resulting trigram to form a hexagram. We also remember from page 109 how the old Taoists divided the Tao by using two spinning wheels, the earlier and later heavenly arrangements. Why were the trigrams doubled and why were they called earlier and later?

The double, 'earlier' and 'later' quality of process structures are crucial aspects of the hexagrams. These qualities remind me of the Hopi Indian categories of 'that which is manifest' and 'that which is beginning to be manifest' and refer to what I call primary and secondary processes. The primary process is 'earlier' than the secondary one in the sense that the primary one is now 'manifest,' it is closer to present awareness than secondary processes which are beginning to manifest. They exist now on the fringe of awareness and will become focal interests in the near future.

Moreover, the primary or earlier processes have the quality of the earlier heaven arrangement (see page 109), which is composed of patterns which are relatively stable. Secondary processes are like the 'later heaven' which is constructed according to the periodic changes in the days and seasons.

## An example

Consider a woman who is so busy that she barely has time to sleep. She is in an existential panic about life, and arrives in my office out of breath, late for our appointment. After telling me about how she was held up by traffic and about all that she has to do, she begins to support her head with a hand while resting her elbow on the arm of the chair. Her primary process, the one she is aware of and the one which is relatively stable is her identity with her busy life. Her secondary process appears first in the form of the traffic jam which held her up and in the form of the arm-head signal which lies at the fringe of her awareness and which is now beginning to manifest. I recommend to her to let me hold her head and to experience more exactly what her head was doing. She says, 'Oh, what a pleasure just to let go and to be supported!' Then I recommended that she use her supporting arm to hold my head. She said, 'Yes, I can support the need to let go' and then she did and began to meditate. This quiet meditation was the secondary process implicit in the recurring traffic jam and arm–head signal.

Her overall pattern was composed of a primary process connected to rushing and a secondary one consisting of double body signals and outer world phenomena which were attempting to transform the primary one by doing things in a more centered way.

### COUPLING WITHIN THE ARCHETYPE

Thus what Jung called archetypes and what the *I Ching* refers to as hexagrams appear to be very differentiated process structures. These structures are self-creating, they arise spontaneously, express themselves in a multitude of channels, have primary and secondary time characteristics which appear earlier and later in awareness, and have secondary processes with a repetitive nature. The *I Ching* continues to differentiate process structures by referring to the coupled nature of the 'lines,' or channels of expression.

The book refers to 'holding together,' and to 'correspondence' between the lines of the individual trigrams which themselves are connected as 'heaven' and 'earth.' The overall significance of the lines is derived according to their 'place' and their coupling to other lines.[4] The relationship between the lines is further differentiated as 'members of a family.'

The coupling between the individual lines of a hexagram corresponds in process science to the coupled connections between the phenomena occurring in different channels. We know from preceding work that these connections lead to concepts such as the dreambody and dream universe and that the invariant aspect of the coupling is called process logic. In other words, the streams of our perception comprise a sort of family of observations connected by the meaning of the overall pattern.

The *I Ching* does not reduce and separate the hexagram into its parts but understands the coupling of the lines in terms of the meaning of the whole. This means that a given 'mysterious' coupling between channels can be understood not simply in terms of the causal connections between them but in terms of the overall pattern. For example, psychosomatic medical processes, parapsychological phenomena such as psychokinesis or levitation, synaesthesia and sychronicity can be comprehended in terms of the relationship between the individual channels of these phenomena and the overall situation of the observer.

Synaesthesia occurs frequently in process-oriented body work where channels overlap and intermingle. In synaesthesia, one might hear with the skin, see with the bones, sense pressure with the eyes and thus mix auditory, visual and proprioceptive channels. Such experiences look very strange at first inspection because we expect seeing, hearing and feeling to operate in association with eyes, ears and proprioceptive receivers, respectively. Our expectations standardize the way in which our perception normally functions and lead to confusion when they do not function in a standard way!

Process logic reduces much of synaesthesia's mystery by looking at the overall picture of a person who experiences an intermingling in the channels. In this picture the individual might appear too organized, too predetermining, and too logical in the way he has been living. We can almost predict that such an individual will experience mixing or overlapping of channels in order to relativize his state-oriented consciousness and introduce him to the fact that nature is more than he expected.

Psychokinesis, or moving objects at a distance, also antagonizes our normal expectations of matter and psyche. However, every therapist has experienced at one time or another what it is like to be physically moved by a patient to do something as if under the influence of that patient. Voodooers and black magicians have been busy with psychokinesis since the beginning of time. If, however, one looks at the dreams of the therapist or those of the patient, then one sees that a given archetype may be constellated which dreams up the environment.

The *I Ching*'s logic may be used to unravel the significance of a group Tao by understanding each member of the group as a specific channel just as a given person's archetypal situation is composed of his individual channels. Thus the group's members are its channels.

For example, family life may be understood as if the family were an individual composed of the events happening within each of its members. Process science then predicts that each member and his relationship to other members of the family are coupled processes whose meaning is finally unraveled only by examining the overall process of the family at any given time. Analogically speaking troubled members of a family or couples of a community forced to undergo unusual processes become the 'moving lines' of a group archetype so to speak, the charged channels whose development is dreamed up and belongs to the evolution of the entire community.

## LIBERATION

Thus, the *I Ching* indicates that the phenomena occurring in a given individual or group channel are coupled together through the overall pattern created by the composition of channels. The implication of the ancient book is that liberation or enlightenment occurs through divining this pattern and adjusting oneself to the overall flow. The process formulation of this implication is that individuation means perceiving and following the structure behind the body phenomena, dreams, relationships and worldly difficulties.

The problem with the *I Ching*'s philosophy is that it is almost impossible to follow!

In practical everyday life processes often occur in exactly those areas which are most antagonistic to consciousness.[5] The saint represses his sexuality, the adult refuses his jealousy and anger. The simplest, human, natural phenomena are often too much for most of us to accept. Nature is complete but we are one-sided and filter out what we perceive.

Thus freedom and liberation are fraught with frustration because following secondary processes takes us to the very edge of our abilities and philosophies. We need time, patience and often help from our friends in becoming aware of our totality. Often we fall backwards in fright and tiredness in the face of our total reality. Liberation from a cyclical rut, a symptom or complex is no simple matter and does not usually occur without a very courageous consciousness or unless a life and death struggle which shoves us over our edges, our conscious reservations. The *I Ching* realized these difficulties centuries ago and warned us that:

> the changes have no consciousness, no action; they are quiescent and do not move. But if they are stimulated, they penetrate all situations under heaven. If they were not the most divine thing on earth, how could they do this.[6]

Here our ancient divinator guide to process work reminds us that the process or present situation in which you live will not change by itself. It needs 'stimulation' and awareness. It needs amplification, we would say. And then process moves, it changes and the worst rut, impasse, symptom and complex can be 'penetrated.' The *I Ching* tells us that this is the 'most divine thing', which means that there is some sort of god experience, a type of religious and wondrous thing, in processes which we cannot grasp without experiencing it. But people have an edge against such experience!

It seems to me as if the weakest point in Taoism is that it does not deal with the edge. The legendary Lao Tsu, author of the *Tao Te Ching*, wrote down his wisdom, for example after most of his edges were crossed, just at the point when he was about to resign from life irritated at the lack of awareness typical of the human condition.[7] Some gate keeper in western China apparently stopped him from leaving the city and dying in the desert for long enough to get him to write his concept of the Tao. He says in chapter 21 of his work *Tao Te Ching* that:

> The greatest virtue is to follow the Tao and Tao alone.
> The Tao is elusive and intangible.
> Oh, it is intangible and elusive and yet within is image.
> Oh, it is elusive and intangible yet within is form.
> Oh, it is dim and dark, and yet within is essence.
> This essence is very real, and therein lies faith.
> From the very beginning until now its name has been forgotten, Thus I perceive the creation.[8]

Lao Tsu reminds us that it is very difficult to discover the Tao; he says it is very real and very tangible, but does not tell us 'how' to discover the Tao. It is important to note that the answer to this 'how' may lie in this story of his writing. Taoist philosophy appears at the point of death!!

The Zen master, Wu Tzu, balances Lao Tsu by stressing that extreme and dangerous circumstances teach the existence of the Tao. He tells a tale which goes something like this.[9] Once there was a boy who earnestly wanted to learn how to be a burglar like his father. The latter, interested in the boy's development, took him on his first 'job' to a rich man's house in the neighborhood. The father-son team broke stealthily in by night, found the treasure chest and opened it. But as the boy stood in front of the the box marveling at its contents, the father quickly shoved him in and locked the chest. Then the old man ran from the house, slamming the door behind him purposely awakening all of its sleeping members. The boy, lacking air and fearing death, scratched like a mouse at the walls of the chest until a curious maid heard the noise and fearfully opened its cover.

Lo and behold! The boy sprang forth like the wind, put out the maid's candle and ran for the door. As he passed the well in the garden he paused for a moment, picked up a stone from the ground and threw it into the water. The family, pursuing the thief, heard the splash and assumed that the thief had drowned.

When the boy got home he asked the father why he locked him in the chest. Instead of answering, the father only inquired about how the boy got away. After hearing the tale he complimented his son on having learned the thief's art.

Wu Tzu implies that tension between life and death is required to learn how to follow the Tao, or to become an enlightened person. This implication is very familiar to me from my practice. Years of training, belief or psychotherapy are not sufficient to help one overcome one's fears of or blocks to perception.

Consider the middle-aged man who had a lung tumor. I had been working with him regularly for some time in a most undramatic fashion. Now the fear of death impelled him, he explained, to get over his 'reservations'. We had touched upon breathing problems earlier, but for some reason the moment did not impell us to really get down to the root of his difficulty.

He began by telling me the following story. He had had a non-malignant tumor removed from his lungs some years ago. Now it had returned to the same spot. This time, his question was, should he operate on it again or not. 'Perhaps it is malignant?' he giggled. We worked with the giggle and he admitted that he felt as if he had regressed. He felt he should not need help even though he did! While he spoke he put his hand on his chest and said that when he felt his impeded breathing experience he saw someone pressing him. I switched channels with him and recommended that he look more closely at his vision. Then his arms moved slightly imitating a sort of hug as he described his vision. I switched to movement and amplified his arm motion by strongly hugging him. As I pressed another memory suddenly reappeared. 'When I was a kid, two friends squeezed me until I fainted! But when I awoke, the world was completely in order!!' He thought a moment and then cried. He admitted for the first time that he was an alcoholic, secretly drinking every day. He spoke of the way he loved 'passing out' and how useful drinking was to him. It enabled him to deal with painful situations. I heard what I guessed must be his passing out in his low tone of voice, and suggested he listen to his voice, leave the words out, and then hum the tone he heard in himself. He began humming and immediately fell into a trance. A moment later he came out of it and slowly said, 'Why operate? Now I am well! Wow, did I need a tumor and chronic breathing problem to get to this state?'

The enlightened Taoist, it seems to me, can be any person who is not only fascinated by the idea of following the processes but who also has the great luck to have a father who sets up the prerequisites for learning or a life with enough trouble, danger and fear to force even a stubborn person to become flexible and aware.

# Chapter 9
# THE ALCHEMICAL OPUS

The alchemist, like the Taoist, also believed that process contained its own solution. He discovered and defined processes in his laboratory, amplified them and marveled at the transformations which miraculously occurred. Like the Taoist, he also got stoned on his work and claimed that it cured everything and healed all problems. He exclaimed that it helped him to transcend death and even spoke of channels which overlapped and amalgamated. Such labora-

6   An Alchemist and his laborant at work, c. 1530 (Mary Evans Picture Library)

tory workers existed and even exist today. Their work is referred to as the 'Opus.'

Their science, alchemy, is probably the oldest science in the world. It has been practiced universally wherever advanced civilizations existed, and mixed in with prevailing religious beliefs. For example, the Chinese Taoists practiced alchemy. They coupled alchemy together with meditation procedures and tried to transform material objects as well as their own physiology.[1] They were interested in becoming subtle bodies which lived forever. The Taoist alchemist saw his own person as the 'prima materia' and cooked it under the controlled fires of his breathing.

We find alchemy also in India intermixed with hatha yoga, tantra and shamanism.[2] Alchemy in Egypt centered on creating immortality.[3] Here, body work was intimately connected with preserving the dead body. Most Arab nations were interested in gold making.[4] The Greeks borrowed laboratory techniques from Egyptian alchemy, added religious philosophy and were the forerunners of the European traditions which I shall focus on in this chapter.

Alchemy reached its peak in medieval Europe but fell upon hard times with the rise of natural science. Jung rediscovered alchemy in the twentieth century and showed that it was the forgotten mother of modern medicine, psychology and physics. He applied the alchemist's laboratory or 'shoptalk' to the transformations of the personality and showed that the *prima materia* was a symbol for the unconscious and that the process of creating gold mirrored individuation.[5]

**THE OPUS**

Now, like the alchemist, I want to drop my theories and talk about practice. I want to speak to the experimental process worker in this chapter. I want to make him feel at home in the 'shoptalk' of alchemy. I am going to use this ancient science in order to help the process worker express his psychotherapeutic psycho-physical labors more completely. In what follows I am going to speak directly to you, dear reader, as though you were a process worker and show you that what you are practicing is a modern version of the most ancient science known to us. If Taoism is your theory, alchemy is your art.

What do you do when you go to your laboratory? Sometimes you feel like playing but mostly you are bound to be gripped by something more serious. Your work may be on yourself, or it may be concerned with someone else, with a couple, a group, a punching bag or a piece of unmolded clay. But whatever it is, a work presents itself to you.

7   *The opus (Biblioteca Apostica Vaticana)*

The alchemist experienced his work similarly and called it the 'opus.'[6] He had various ideas about what it must be but never formulated this work exactly because, like the process worker, the method interested him more than the result most of the time.

### SOLVE ET COAGULA

He had his own shoptalk of course. As he sat in front of his flasks and bottles, his fires and vapors, he heard his unconscious whispering into his ear the famous alchemical secrets, 'Solve et Coagula,' and 'Solvite corpora et coagulate spiritum.'[7]

Dissolve the body and coagulate the spirit. 'Switch channels,' he must have thought. See if a body problem can bring insight or if a dream can be expressed kinesthetically! The alchemist apparently was interested in volatilizing the concrete and concretizing fantasy.

He imagined his 'opus' to be a stone. In fact he called the goal of his work the 'philosopher's stone.' If you are a process worker, you will understand him when he tells you that his goal was the philosopher's stone and that his method was (watch out for the switch here!) the 'stone of the philosophers.'[8] I do not think that he meant to be confusing, for only a theorist would be confused here at the reversal of method and goal.

The alchemist's goal was his method! The alchemist was like you, dear process worker. He was not primarily interested in creating the cure-all like modern psychotherapists striving for the panacea. The true alchemist was someone who was his destination, so to speak. You will understand him, I am sure. He tried to follow processes and realized that when he succeeded in following nature nothing more was required. His opus was his method, the attitude of religiously following nature.

The paradox is that the way is the goal. This paradox conforms to your experience. You have noticed, I am sure, that people repeatedly meet with old problems regardless of what sort of psychotherapy they use. The happiest of them are not the ones who have made birch trees out of maple trees, who have solved their problems or changed themselves but the ones who got birch saplings to grow respectfully into birch trees. Their goal was the never ending process of unfolding.

### THE *PRIMA MATERIA*

Don't you sometimes get embarrassed when your neighbor asks you what you do? What can you tell them? If you are a process worker, you never know what you are going to do before you get into your laboratory. Other professions can

8  *An alchemist at work 1544 (Mary Evans Picture Library)*

be clear. But if you are too exact you are not a process worker! Sometimes you help kids learn to read better, sometimes you work on a back tumor, at other times you spend an hour crying yourself, then there are periods of nervous embrace, deep breathing, dream work, lecturing like a minister, recommending diets, being silent for the day. One hour you work like a poet; the next like an auto mechanic. Who is going to understand all this? To begin with you can tell the neighbors that you work with people or problems and hopefully this explanation will suffice.

The alchemist would blandly say when your neighbor asks what he does, that he is doing his 'opus,' working on the *prima materia.*' If the neighbor were impertinent enough to ask what this was, then the alchemist would uninhibitedly speak chemical poetry. He did not live in the latter part of the twentieth century.!

The *prima materia,*' he would say, is a 'constant soul' and also an 'imperfect body' which may be found buried underground in a mine.[9] The time to dig for it depends upon the horoscope. This statement will quiet the neighbor, I am sure.

But you understand the alchemist immediately. The *prima materia*' is another word for the beginning of a process. Why did the alchemist not call his process the Tao or the Time? Well, he almost did when he said that you could find the *prima materia*' only when the horoscope indicated the moment had arrived to begin an opus. The alchemist, however, stressed the *materia*' aspect of processes, while the ordinary Taoist was concerned with the structure of events around him. The European alchemist experienced processes mainly in his pots and pans. The Taoist was a proprioceptive visual type, a philosopher, the alchemist basically a visual kinesthetic person. He would have loved body work and certainly have been fascinated by experimental physics!

However, the alchemist was not materialistic. He did say after all that the *prima materia* had a 'constant soul.'[10] You know what he meant? He implied that the processes he worked with were perseverating (i.e. constant) events. He would not simply have attacked the first itch he saw, but would have waited to see if the itch perseverated, if it had continuity. He waited to see which processes repeated and these he worked on.

He said quite clearly that the *'prima materia'* was an 'imperfect body' by which he meant that it had to be perfected. It began by being impure, incomplete and in need of transformation. Any ordinary tumor, itch, anxiety, headache or stroke of fate is an 'imperfect body' asking to be cooked and transformed. Fantasies and tics are 'imperfect' because they are not congruent with the rest of the personality. The *prima materia* transforms to perfection by unifying all of its separate, incongruent and disharmonious parts, by focusing simultaneously on primary and secondary processes.

### THE *IGNIS NONNATURALIS*

I am sure that your neighbor will have stopped the conversation by this time. But if you get together with other process workers, and talk 'shop,' one of them is bound to mention that 'things happen by themselves.' An alchemist would help you express yourself more exactly by saying that there is an *'ignis nonnaturalis,'*[11] a natural spark in processes which makes them evolve.

You get excited at this point because you too have seen this *'ignis.'* You often observed that you need not put much energy into the work because the energy is already there. Each incongruent process has its own *'ignis.'* Here is a 'new' term for your shoptalk!

Recall the man who began his work by rubbing his brow. Recall how you amplified his rubbing and how the rubbing energy transformed into visions and active imaginations. The amplified *ignis* transformed the kinesthetic channel into vision. Remember the woman who complained about always being turned on? You encouraged her to experience her *'ignis'* and she felt immediately whole. You were afraid she would attack you sexually and were surprised when her excitement became her life dance. Proprioceptive energy turned into movement! Thank god!

The alchemist described his *'ignis nonnaturalis'* as a 'dry water which does not wet the hands,' and also as a 'fire which does not burn'[12] and you know just why he said this. He had to because he was so amazed that the processes he observed, the wild fires he experienced, did not harm anyone. You too have seen many sexual impulses go the way of tantric yoga in the sense of switching channels or becoming integrated as whole experiences without burning anyone. How many fits have you seen in which people banged on your punching bag, screamed at their parents and teachers without ever having even scratched themselves in the process? How much water have you seen which did not wet, how many tears which did not drown the person but brought him to a state of enlightenment? Amazing, but in the many hundreds of hours you have watched the *prima materia* doing its own opus with the help of the '*ignis nonnaturalis,*' you have never once seen an injury—to date at least—which exceeded a scratched elbow or bruised fist. Apparently people are less dangerous to themselves when they are doing process work than when they are letting out their affects without awareness.

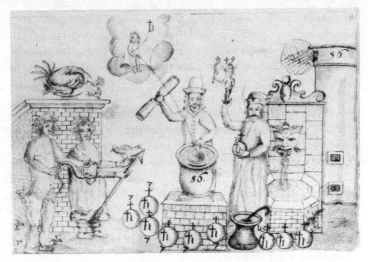

9   *The oven and the egg (Biblioteca Apostica Vaticana)*

**THE EGG**

Once you find the *prima materia* and discover that it has its
own energy, say in a tense back, a moving finger, a stroke of
fate or a vision, you put the *prima materia* into an egg, a
'philosopher's egg.'[13] 'Philosopher' meant for the alchemist
a 'lover of wisdom', and egg meant literally a place to grow.

Even if you may not have loved your academic background, you may still be a philosopher if you are a lover of
wisdom. In fact, if you are a process worker, you have to be
a philosopher because you guide your own life by a form of
wisdom which is greater than any you may have learned;
the process itself.

This is why you undertake the opus in the first place. You
need to discover and know. If you knew how to lead your
life you would not have anything to do with this form of
work, unless of course you were simply a mad experi-
mentalist. But such madness is foreign to you. You are not
interested in science for science's sake but for your own
human use. That is why you focus on the *prima materia* in a
loving way and thereby create an egg in which it can
develop. The egg encircles the *prima materia* and singles it
out as the work. First you define the *prima materia* as a
process buried underground at quite a distance from
consciousness in one of the double or triple non-congruent
signals of the personality. Then you wait until the process
perseverates demonstrating its own '*ignis nonnaturalis*,' and
then, bang! You hermetically seal this inside an egg by
intensely focusing on it with all your heart, waiting for the
process to transform. Your egg is your commitment to the
process, your conscious attitude which says, 'I trust
whatever is in my focus, I believe it will bring me whatever
it is I am supposed to discover about this life.'

But since the philosopher's egg is also just a simple egg, it
is a piece of nature not created by man, and is thus not a
product of the will. The egg symbolizes a property which
most people have, a natural focus, attention or interest
which brings creative sparks to birth, which unfolds the
essence of your person.

The essence of this spark is known to everyone. Something put you on this earth in the first place, something is keeping you alive, and something is unfolding this spark into the evolution of your life. People forget about the origins of life, however, and do not feel, see or hear it in themselves.

Process work brings one back into contact with this spark because it depends upon your dreams, body and outer situation. The Taoists focused on that crazy little spark which puts dreams into your head, which makes you aware of fantasies, which moves your body in this direction or that, and which creates internal dialogue with the unfathomable spirit.

Thus the egg is the capacity to pick up this spark and carry it to its conclusion, to listen to internal dialogue, to care for fantasies, to notice your body motions and follow them. The alchemist as a philosopher or lover of wisdom differentiated himself from others. 'Having a process' in a conscious way is a very unusual thing. Most people are not very interested in becoming lovers of their process wisdom. Others might be interested but are led away from their processes. The horde of teachers, psychologists and physicians tell these people that their processes are wrong and try to get them to change themselves, to get rid of their problems and their symptoms.

Thus we learn other people's wisdom, fit ourselves into eggs which do not belong to us and do not arrive at the point where we have our own process. We may find temporary solutions to our griefs and symptoms but do not get around to solving the larger, and central human problem: learning how to have a process, mother the inner spark of life which put us on this planet and which sends us back to wherever we came from.

### THE OVEN

Following alchemical tradition, you put the egg in 'Athanor,' the oven which is devised to keep the process at constant temperature over long periods of time.[14] Until now, your work has been mainly observation. You had to find the *prima materia*, single it out, seal it off and divide it from all other things in a loving way.

Now, the work changes. You must begin cooking. By studying amplification and practicing it on body processes, dream images, strokes of fate, and relationship problems you have in fact created a man-made object, an oven. You know just how important this oven can be. If you heat things up too much with amplification, if you push something more than its nature allows, you can split the opus in the egg to pieces and may even get hit by the parts. You can lose your commitment!

Have you not heard stories from your colleagues about therapists who were too ambitious and who did not follow the process of their clients? Remember the therapist who broke a client's resistance, opened her up too early with body work and did not respect her character armour? He left her defenseless and she was subsequently attacked on a New York street and almost killed. A good story to remember when you think it is your job to push things farther than they want to go.

On the other hand, how many times has your oven functioned without enough heat? You were too shy to step in on something, and things went cold and died. Your client went to another therapist who was more real and direct than you. Indeed, keeping things at a constant temperature which is neither too hot nor too cold is difficult. You have to constantly check the process by looking through the little window in your oven to get the necessary information to see if things are too hot or too cold. You need to listen to the client's voice, watch his posture, observe his eyes to see how things are going.

### THE PUFFERS

When you have a bad day you turn into a 'puffer' and blow like hell through your bellows, impatient that the oven will not bring the *prima materia* in the philosopher's egg quickly enough to completion. You should throw in your towel, go home and rest. Otherwise you will turn into your shadow, the puffer:

He knows, he claims the means to accrue within one's own home the mother lode of all treasures, without any other riches than that of a part of those one possesses. On the strength of his words . . . one succumbs, one sows one's gold to reap but smoke. . . . There are few artists who are true alchemists. . . . True alchemists do not glory in their science; they do not seek to swindle or cheat other people out of their money because . . . he that has everything, needs nothing . . .[15]

The puffer, in short, is the power shadow of psychology, the one who claims to achieve wondrous effects and who identifies himself with creation itself. Beware. Process work is so much fun and creates so much numen that if you are not careful you will either think too much of yourself or else suffer from inferiority when you lose your ability to follow and respect the process. You push. Watch out! The *prima materia* is full of poisons. Remember that you can be dreamed up by blocked clients to puff too much. Let people do their own work. But alas, few people are prepared—in the beginning at least—to discover their own process. And many have little '*ignis.*'

### STAGES OF TRANSFORMATION

Now the work begins. The alchemist peeks into his oven and what does he see? CONFLICT!!

I am sure he did not always see a fiery conflict. But he saw it so many times that he assumed that conflict was the beginning of transformation of the *prima materia*. The solar, hot and male principle (sulphur) attacked the lunar cold female essence (mercury) and all hell broke loose.[16]

How many times have you seen process work begin with a conflict? Sometimes people tell you they are in conflict with others. At other times they tell you they do not like even you. (Then the two of you are in the pot.) Sometimes their bodies are in tension and their conflicts are somatized. Remember the case of the neck tumor? (last chapter) There, the male principle was the strangler the 'sun', and the lunar principle was the weak ego. When you work on headaches you often find a powerful solar force straining against a lethargic lunar mercuriality which needs awakening. How many cramps turned out to be arousers in which solar power was trying to awaken an easy-going, quiet, lunar personality? Any incongruent signal is in conflict with awareness. Primary and secondary double signals do not get along in part because no one paid the double signals much respect before.

## THE *AQUA PERMANENS*

As long as things are in conflict, everything is tense. But after focusing on this conflict, processes move out of the realm of opposites. They literally kill or exhaust one another. The alchemist looking into his pots imagined the solar and the lunar principles fighting to extinction.

You know what this is like. You begin with one extreme, one polarity in process work, let it move or speak for itself, and then another extreme becomes activated and begins to fight. After a while, they begin to amalgamate or flip into one another so that they become indistinguishable. The angry father sounds like the little boy, the helpless child turns into a powerful god. The aggressive fists of the puncher turn into the fluttering chest of wailing depression. The opposites annihilate each other or become indistinguishable as flow takes the place of polarity.

The alchemists called this flow the 'aqua permanens', or permanent water.[17] *Aqua permanens* is the fluid process, the energy or life which was locked up in the tension of conflict which has now been freed through the flow between the opposites. Fluidity comes from conflict. Whereas before there was a boundary between conflicting opposites, between intent and reality, streaming energy now transforms therapy into natural science.

## THE NIGREDO

That moment in which the opposites disappear and in which the liquid of life arises is called the *nigredo*, 'the darkness darker than dark,' the 'black of blacks.'[18] Strangely enough the alchemist claims that this is the 'first sign that (he) is on the right path.' He said that there is 'no generation without corruption.'[19]

You as a process worker will be surprised about the alchemists' positive attitude towards the *nigredo*, because you know how many hours you have sat wondering about the loss of consciousness which takes place when people leave their known primary process! The 'black of blacks' is *exactly* that, and anyone who has followed processes through the *nigredo* will know that this darkening is something which requires the deepest respect and also fear.

Don't puff! You often wonder why many people in practical work stop their processes at the solution to the opposites. In fact, this is where state-oriented psychology, which created therapies in order to create solutions, came from in the first place. Conflicts arise, and then solutions and then goodbye—see you next week. The same conflicts arise again—and new solutions appear and so forth. Not everyone must go on beyond the opposites, beyond revealing the existence of a conflict.

I am impressed with Jung, who, in the year 1913, so painfully deliberated over his first active imagination and finally let himself fall into that imaginary visual in his fantasy world.[20] I recall the warning of Don Juan to deliberate well before entering the nagual. First the apprentice must become a hunter, then learn the exact and controlled methods of the warrior before letting go and controlling his abandon.[21] I have read many Zen texts about teachers who recommended to their pupils to stay with the opposites, to hold on to given moral rules and disciplines, to refrain from sex, eat vegetables and go to bed early after meditating.[22] These mores are something different from ordinary dogmatic religious principles. They are channels and opposites meant to hold the apprentice together until the moment arrives when he can leave the channels which consciousness has identified itself with and move on into other worlds.

The approach to the *nigredo* is thus not a matter of the will but a process which is lengthy and sometimes life-long. Some reach it only at the moment of death itself and indeed, there have been many dying processes which I have witnessed which seemed to center around the need to annihilate the opposites, enter the *nigredo* and become fluid. In any case, there is no sense in puffing towards the *nigredo*. I say this because many therapies are developing today which feel that their job consists in bringing people to the point of the nagual and then returning them again. They have many 'good' recommendations like bang on the floor or beat on a rug with a rubber hose! Each to his own.

The process worker knows how many people go to the stage of opposites and stop. That is the end, for the moment, at least. But there is also another type of process which continues. This process phase frequently is presaged by comments such as, 'I am losing my orientation,' or 'I do not know where I am.' Sometimes process returns to the land of the opposites in order to gather more control. A wild trip without a pilot usually brings nothing but a lot of excitement. An uncontrolled journey leaves one feeling empty afterwards.

However, there are others who, after long studies, because of fateful stress or because of inner need, are pressed to abandon themselves in a controlled way to their own inner rulership of their process. I have seen many such processes occur, some can be described, others are unmentionable. Some spin through space without knowing where they will land, others make weird noises, hum strange tunes and enact unthinkable body postures. A few look like trance shamans learning to develop awareness in new spaces and to contact foreign beings. Others suffer untold misery and uncertainty, mistaking their wandering for insanity.

People who have prepared themselves typically relive well-known archetypal processes experienced for thousands of years by alchemists, shamans and medicine men. If you know about these processes, you are able to sit back and let nature happen. If you are not informed about these ancient processes, have not read about shamanism, studied yoga, gone on vision quests or simply lived enough yourself, then you will block such processes from happening because you are afraid of the unknown.

*An example*
I remember one very strong confrontation with the *nigredo*.
A client came to me because of periodic psychotic episodes
which began during some workshop she had attended in
which breathing exercises had been used. My client was a
visual type and therefore focusing upon her unoccupied
proprioception in breathing flipped her. Even as she told me
about how terrible her previous psychotic states were, she
began to access past memories and breathe deeply with loud
gasps punctuated by distressed facial signals asking for
help. She whispered 'and then I lost all sense of my
movement on this planet and fell unconscious.' As she said
this, her body began to vibrate so violently from head to foot
that I told her (using her main channel and last statement
about movement) 'Look at your body, and move the
movements, follow the movements you see there!' This
recommendation helped her. She jittered and vibrated with
awareness and said, after two or three moments, 'You
know, I am shaking because my body gets cold when I leave
this planet.' 'Settle the problems you have here, work on the
warmth-coldness issue before leaving,' I suggested and she
immediately began talking about relationship problems.
    My client fell into the *nigredo* because she began occupy-
ing a channel in which she had little awareness. She needed
to learn more about body feeling, about love and hate before
dropping her intellect and drowning in the *nigredo*.
    Switching channels is a violent act. It is as therapeutic as it
may be dangerous. When it happens spontaneously, time
can be a devil, or else the only therapist. However, how
long one remains in the *nigredo* and how one fares there also
depends, in my experience, upon the therapist's ability and
the client's awareness in unoccupied channels.
    There is no doubt, however, that deep transformative
experiences usually pass through the *nigredo* because in this
state, in the unoccupied channel, lies the weak link holding
up the personality, the inferior function, the treasure in the
mine, and the missing information in consciousness. I
suspect that learning how to deal with the altered states of
consciousness, with the experience of secondary processes

and the temporary darkening of the primary process will be the task for psychology for a long time to come.

## MERCURY OF THE WISE

Look! Something is happening in the egg! The *nigredo*, like the night sky, is suddenly punctuated and illuminated by a 'starry aspect,' a constellation referred to as 'Mercury of the Wise.'[23] The stars were considered by the alchemist to be directions from within the *prima materia* itself. The star indicated to him that a new child was born, signifying a sense of guidance from a distant source of wisdom.

But, you, dear process worker, have seen this too. The black of blacks only seems like a starless night in the first moment. As you become accustomed to wandering outside the lighted area a new director variously called 'personal power,' or the ally, the self or dreambody wisdom directs one as a star in the night.

In practical work, the stars appear as sudden visions or as the impulse to perform certain body postures. In the previous example, the body's shaking was the star in the night. At other times, the stars may appear as a form of extrasensory perception, or even as a synchronicity.

In any case, the stars in the alchemist's symbolism refer to a birth or rebirth of their 'divine child.' The new thing which is born or discovered is wisdom implicit in processes themselves. Until now one has had to govern life according to learned and conscious principles. And now, one knows that one can let go because a 'personal power,' or a special ally is at hand. One can afford to let go because awareness of the 'star' inhibits one from falling into oblivion. The ground principle of life itself is the inner directness of one's own process, a new earth, the alchemists would say which supports one in the darkness. Perhaps this was the *nigredo*'s purpose in the first place. One had to die in order to discover a new life principle.

## THE PEACOCK'S TAIL

The advent of the starry stuff on the surface of the liquid *nigredo* signals that the dark of darks is coming to an end and that a new phase is beginning. Out of the destruction of the opposites comes a new volatile principle which is strikingly like the old one. The alchemists fantasized that from the earth a bird arises like a flash, trying to free itself from the gravitational pull of the earth. Failing, it falls again and again onto the 'new earth' and is amalgamated by it. During the flying up and plummeting down, many colors appear which the alchemist called the 'peacock's tail.'[24]

The image of the bird flying away from and landing on the 'new earth' symbolizes the process immediately following the *nigredo*. Many people coming out of the *nigredo* feel that their work is finished. They will even say, 'well, thank you,' try to get up from the floor, rise out of their 'samahdi' and return to the place they came from. But their eyelids seem unwilling to open, their body only rises halfheartedly, their limbs no longer obey the commands from the chakra between the eyes because a new earth, a new power, has pulled the spirit back where it came from.

Like a metal filing unable to leave its magnetic field the regenerated primary process is drawn into the field of the secondary one. In fact, the opus is just beginning a second and even further stage of process work. At this point different types of exclamations appear, such as, 'Wow, I have not even experienced this on an LSD trip and I seem to be going on yet for more,' or 'I want to get up but I get dizzy if I move. Something pulls me back.'

These exclamations are the colorful reactions occurring as one tries to fly back to where one came from but is caught by the tenacity of the process itself. The process has become so strong that it attracts and involves ego focus. The ego for its part has been transformed, and now, relieved of its command, feels secure in the existence of another power. Happy, it returns to the new earth. Ordinary life was anyhow not so interesting.

### THE *ALBEDO*
Sometimes the peacock's tail goes on for a long time during which integrating experiences of the unconscious are taking place. Often quiet periods ensue in which nothing seems to

be happening from the outside. But inside a gradual whitening is occurring which the alchemist calls the '*albedo*.'[25] He said that at this stage of the work, the *prima materia* was strong enough to withstand destruction.

Empirical observations of individuals who have proceeded beyond the *nigredo* show that the eyes both figuratively and literally open by themselves. The individual might say (when asked later) that he awakened as if from a dream, as if the dawn were coming.

Eye phenomena are useful process signs. The eyes close when there is too much light. Often other channels are trying to open up when the eyes close. Proprioceptive experiences or even visions which have not been allowed to exist can now happen. The eyes close in part to decrease relationship contact with the outer world, to hear what is happening within or to experience breathing, heart rate, energy variations and fatigue. The eyes close in order to become inner directed. Children will often shut their eyes when they feel danger is coming because reality for them is visual-outward. Adults look away when they are in danger of losing their own processes to the outer world.

In the *albedo* however, the eyes gradually open and actually give rise to the visual experience of whitening. Coincident with the opening of the eyes and focusing on the people and places where one is, are a nod of the head and insights such as 'so this is what has been missing in my life,' or 'that is what was wrong before.' Along with these insights the noise of the world is heard again replacing the sound of inner tones. Real objects appear to melt with inner visions as one moves over a dreaming threshold. Sensations move from proprioceptive and visceral experiences to the large muscles and movement.

These signals tell us that the first stage of the deep-sea journey in process work is drawing to a close. Awakening is an autonomous power. Altered states of consciousness and unused channels fluidly switch into the world as one knew it before.

## CONJUNCTIO

At this point, process scientist, you probably pack up your supplies, clean your office, and prepare to go home. You say goodbye to your starry-eyed companion with whom you shared a secret drama and with whom you now feel at home.

State-oriented reality meets you once again and with it a not altogether surprising insight occurs. The process is still unfinished. Even though you may have hoped that the *albedo* had prepared the individual to withstand the tension of time, in fact, you learn that this is not the case. Processes are replaced once again by insensitivity and unconsciousness. Insight, experience, special promises to oneself and feelings which occurred during the *albedo* do not remain. They drift away as if they were a dream.

But, alas, this too is part of the process. Your office was but a flask, a measure of reality but no substitute for the world. Completion happens only during the last phase of the work, the *'conjunctio'* which is described by the alchemists as the 'king uniting with the queen in the fire of love.[26] From this union only does completion occur in which the stone is born.

The king, according to Jung, symbolizes the alchemical process itself while the queen stands for the servant of the process. She is the loving attitude which supports that which is trying to happen.[27] She is that regal attitude which gives up one's own way in order to amplify the supraordination of fate.

Until now, the process worker and not the client has been the queen. Hence, method and process, receptive and creative or king and queen have not been quite married. True, there may have been isolated moments when method and process were one in your laboratory flask, singular and meaningful times when the client supported his own process. But now, near the end of the opus, method and process are married. As the client grows to appreciate the impossible nature of process, he approaches its spirit of transformation and joins this spirit upon its restless journey. Until now he could afford to examine processes and actually flirt with their energy and wisdom. But now, he finds that he himself has found a relationship to the world of nature and its happenings and can follow them even when their direction seems foreign.

### UNIO MENTALIS

Alchemists like Dorn differentiated the last stage of the alchemical process. He divided the *conjunctio* into three phases and called the first, the *'unio mentalis.'*[28] Jung compares this phase to mental solutions which change one's attitude towards reality. In this state of the work, one realizes the meaning of process, and has insight into its nature. One understands one's dreams but cannot yet live them.

### THE CAELUM

Jung identifies Dorn's second *conjunctio* stage, the *'caelum,'*[29] as mental solutions which are brought together with the physical body. One not only understands process and has an 'ah ha' reaction to it, but simultaneously feels the meaning of things in the body. The *'caelum'* symbolizes that stage of the end of the work in which insight simultaneously occurs with body experience, one dances and has a *'satori'*, an enlightenment, one feels pain and understands the meaning of one's fate.

### UNUS MUNDUS

Dorn differentiated a final state of the *conjunctio* which he called the *'unus mundus,'* the one world in which the *caelum* or mind-body solution was joined with the universe.[30] In the *unus mundus*, all that happened in the flask, in your private office or room happens out here on the city street, in the midst of real, everydaylife.

You know, dear process scientist, just how many mental solutions to problems you have seen and how many mind-body relaxations and congruencies you have witnessed in the confines of your laboratory which fell asunder under the impact of daily life. Surprisingly little of the *unio mentalis* or *caelum* held up under the stress of the social pressure outside your laboratory. The occupation of the world channel seems always to come last.

The stage just preceding the 'unus mundus' is known to all. One works successfully on dreams and body problems but nevertheless melts confluently and unconsciously with the routine streaming of the collective world, adapting to whatever is expected. The body reacts with pain while nightmares shake the night. Personal incongruence is the heavy price paid for following linear time and social pressure. Dreams of walking lonely paths in nature filled the philosophical egg before one dared birth. Now as the final stage of the *conjunctio* nears, old and familiar opponents from the inner world are dreamed up to be the judges at the edge of the land you are leaving. You would like to return to womb-like and familiar territory but something like death pushes you beyond the aging visage of fear.

No one should be naive because total congruence between mind, body and nature does not mean only joy and relaxation. In fact, the opposite may be the case. Since congruence requires relating primary and secondary processes and since secondary processes become double signals when they conflict with consciousness, the more congruent you become the more you transform your own identity and the more you conflict with ruling deities of order which no longer nourish your soul.

Thus, the individual growing towards wholeness dreams up his peers to be misoneistic primitives who reject unpredictable fluidity. Luckily the pain generated by the conflict between secondary processes and common sense is ameliorated by contact with the Tao, the feeling of truth which remains after the old gods have died.

Until now, this truth has been projected onto the wave equations of physics, the potential world of the archetypes, the alchemists, *unus mundus*, mythology's Oceanos, Aion and Kundalini. Now Tao is an experience. It is your ally, an inner certainty related to the overall state of the world which detaches you from the opinions of your group.

Talmudic literature, American Indian tradition and Taoist stories remind you of the powerful and ameliorating effect of this ally.[31] They predict that if one person gets himself together while being in this real world, that the whole world will fall into order. Process theory agrees, for we know that if one channel, one person changes, then the pattern for the rest of us changes as well. If one person is real and honest everyone is relieved! Inversely, it takes one person to be out of himself to disturb a group or one sick group to disturb an individual. Being your total self in the world is an important and difficult task.

## GOLD

Apparently the alchemist's gold, imagined as the finale of his culinary labors, is a complex thing which consists of more than sunshine. This opus was supposed to produce the panacea from the dung heap of human mystery. But no one said much about the difficulties of bearing the tension and pressure, the loneliness and darkness which arise when the individual conflicts with collective patterns. True, process awareness relieves the body of much suffering and even sometimes creates the experience of liberation. But symptoms and problems do not simply disappear, they continue until one is able, for the moment at least, to experience all channels.

Thus the gold turns out to be something different from the yogic super powers, the ability to walk on air, ingest fire or heal wounds. Of course there were mind-boggling channel changes, overlappings, levitations, healings and immortality. But unlike the alchemical puffer who sweated in vain for some sort of LSD trip which would free him from this world, a person in the *unus mundus* loses interest in the original dreams of gold and immortality. Empirical work with the living and dying indicate that increased process awareness obviates future expectations. Such awareness may be the gold. This point is where Taoists, Buddhists, Yogis and modern psychologists meet. The closer you get to the end, the more you realize there is none, unless you are able to consider openness to new challenges as the last step.

# RIVER'S WAY

And so it seems as if the goal of alchemy was in part to find the river's way, that is the process of perception. This makes practical sense because once a person's awareness has been increased to the point where he is able to pick up his own signals alone, his own body feelings, movements, visions, words and vocal tones, he has all that one can give him to go on alone, with or without the love and help of someone else. There seems to be no objective real world 'out there,' no gold for the seeker, no object for the physicist, no dream for the analyst to gain mastery over, to possess, own or manipulate.

However this eastern-sounding conclusion, together with its western counterparts in theoretical physics, does not mean that objective reality does not exist. It means that the discipline, effort and accuracy applied to creating health, peace or wealth can be equally well applied to discovering more about the nature of perception. It implies that when a person complains that he has a stomach ache, you need to find out exactly how he perceives this ache. Is it like a fist, fire, movement or what? When you work with his perception, it changes. Though the sufferer may tell you he feels better, you still do not know what his stomach ache really was. Such questions may be unanswerable. We can only be certain about your and his perceptions.

Much more needs to be understood about this process. In this book I have contented myself with noting that perception is organized according to its channels and distance from consciousness. The flow of the river, the Tao or evolution of our world, is structured according to the patterns of this perception. I was amazed to find process concepts hidden in ancient time and energy deities. Even more thrilling was to find channels and primary and secondary processes in the *I Ching*. I almost expected to find amplification methods and process stages predicted in the alchemist's dreams.

My studies have given me greater respect for history and, at the same time, increased insight into the limitations of alchemy and Taoism. It seems likely that one of the reasons why Taoism has remained more of a theory than a practice is because most of the events Taoism deals with are accidental. They are secondary processes which, like dreams, are hindered by edges from reaching our conscious attention. Questions about what to do next would be alleviated if we could perceive what we are doing now. Until we can perceive this the mystery of Taoism and the magic of alchemy will remain essentially theories without direct applications.

But what will future scientists have to say about the present state of psychology? How close are we to bringing even modern theories of the unfolding universe to earth? I myself wonder what a detailed study of psychotic states is going to do for process work. What will we learn from synchronicity? Until psychology deals with world problems as well as it does with individual ones, the *unus mundus*, Taoist sage and alchemist's gold will remain unrealized dreams of a bygone age.

But most important of all, what will happen to the individual when his ability to perceive increases? If experience is an indicator, increasing ability at picking up signals and courage in working with their implications will liberate the individual from false teachers and healers. Neither knowledge, luck nor intelligence but expanded sensitivity to the wisdom of one's own process creates the independence of a congruent personality.

# NOTES

## CHAPTER 1  INTRODUCTION

1 C.J. Jung, 'Principles of Practical Psychotherapy', Collected Works vol. 16, pp. 3, 4.
2 B.K.S. Iyengar, Light on Yoga, Yoga Dipika (New York: Schocken Books, 1979); Alexander Lowen, Bioenergetics (New York: Coward, McCann & Geoghegan, 1975).
3 Wilhelm Reich, Character Analysis (New York: Farrar, Straus & Giroux, 1968).
4 Moshe Feldenkrais, Body and Mature Behavior (New York: International Universities Press, 1973).
5 Ida Rolf, 'Structural Integration,' Confinaia Psychiatrica XVI (1973), pp. 69-79.
6 Ilsa Weith (translator), The Yellow Emperor's Classic of Internal Medicine (Berkeley, California: University of California Press, 1966).
7 John Niehardt, Black Elk Speaks: Being the Life Story of a Holy Man of the Ogalala Sioux (Nebraska: University of Nebraska Press, 1961).
8 J.L. Moreno, Who Shall Survive? (New York: Beacon Press, 1952); Lewis Yablonsky, Psychodrama (New York: Basic Books, 1976).
9 Barbara Hannah, Active Imagination (Los Angeles: Sigo Press, 1980).
10 Lu K'uan Yu, Taoist Yoga: Alchemy and Immortality (London: Rider & Company, 1972).
11 Fritz Perls, Gestalt Therapy Verbatim (Lafayette, California: Real People Press, 1969).
12 Eric Berne, Beyond Games and Scripts (New York: Grove Press, 1977).
13 Richard Bandler, and John Grinder, Frogs into Princes, Neuro-Linguistic Programming, ed. by John O. Stevens (Moab, Utah: Real People Press, 1979).

14 Adelaide Bry, *A Primer of Behavioral Psychology* (New York: New American Library, 1975).
15 Virginia Satir, *Helping Families to Change* (Hays, Kansas: The High Plains Comprehensive Community Mental Health Center, 1972).
16 C.G. Jung, *Man and His Symbols*, together with M.L. von Franz, Joseph L. Henderson, Jolande Jacobe, Aniela Jaffe (New York: Dell, 1971).
17 C.G. Jung, 'Synchronicity,' *Collected Works*, vol. 8 (London: Routledge & Kegan Paul).

CHAPTER 2 ELEMENTS OF PROCESS SCIENCE

1 See C.G. Jung, 'Psychological Types,' *Collected Works*, vol. 6; and M.L. von Franz, 'The Inferior Function' in von Franz and Hillman, *Lectures on Jung's Typology* (New York: Spring Publications, 1971).
2 *Ibid.*
3 Mindell, *Dreambody* (Boston: Sigo Press, 1981; London: Routledge & Kegan Paul, 1984) and *Working with the Dreaming Body* (London and Boston: Routledge & Kegan Paul, 1985).
4 In the *Dreambody* I concentrate on the connection between visualized dreams and proprioceptive experiences. In *Working with the Dreambody* I integrate dream and body work with practical examples of process theory. *The Global Dreambody* focuses upon channels in family and couple's processes.

CHAPTER 3 DREAM AND BODY CHANNELS

1 Larry Dossey, *Time, Space and Medicine* (Boulder, Col.: Shambhala, 1982).
2 *Ibid.*, pp. 139-41.
3 *Ibid.*, pp. 142-9.
4 D. Bohm, *Wholeness and the Implicate Order* (London: Routledge & Kegan Paul, 1980).
5 A. Mindell, *Working with the Dreaming Body*.

CHAPTER 4 RELATIONSHIP CHANNELS

1 C.G. Jung, 'The Transference,' *Collected Works*, vol. 16.
2 Fritz Perls, *Gestalt Therapy Verbatim* (Lafayette, California: Real People Press, 1969).
3 *Ibid.*
4 Eric Berne, *Beyond Games and Scripts* and Claude Steiner, *Scripts People Live By* (New York: Bantam, 1975).
5 R. Bandler and J. Grinder, *Frogs into Princes* (Moab, Utah: Real

People Press, 1979).

6 A. Bry, *A Primer in Behavioral Psychology* (New York: New American Library, 1975).

7 C.G. Jung, 'The Transference,' *op. cit.*

8 Arnold Mindell, *Working with the Dreaming Body* (London: Routledge & Kegan Paul, 1985). I should also mention here the work of the now Freudian, Thomas Ogden, who in *Projective Identification* refers to projective mechanisms which evoke congruent feelings in others.

9 Jung defines projection in 'Psychological Types', *Collected Works*, vol. 6 (Princeton, New Jersey: Princeton University Press, Bollingen Series XX, 1971); Von Franz, Marie-Louise, *Projection and Reflection in Jungian Psychology* (La Salle, Ill.: Open Court, 1980).

10 Philip Rawson, *Tantra: The Indian Cult of Ecstasy* (London: Thames & Hudson, 1973).

11 Lu K'uan Yu, *Taoist Yoga: Alchemy and Immortality* (London: Rider, 1972).

12 *Ibid.*

13 Rawson, *op. cit.*


CHAPTER 5  WORLD CHANNELS

1 Some of the original papers of these physicists are:
John von Neuman, *The Mathematical Foundations of Quantum Mechanics*, trans. R. Beyer (Princeton, New Jersey: Princeton University Press, 1955); Albert Einstein and L. Infeld, *The Evolution of Physics* (Cambridge, Mass.: Cambridge University Press, 1971); H. Stapp, 'Theory of Reality,' *Foundations of Physics*, 7 (1977); David Finkelstein, 'Quantum Physics and Process Metaphysics,' in *Physical Reality and Mathematical Description*, ed. by Enz and Mehra (Durecht, Holland: D. Reidel, 1974).

2 See Gary Zukav, *The Dancing Wu Li Masters* (London: Rider, 1979); Fritjof Capra, *The Tao of Physics* (London: Wildwood House, 1975); Bob Toben, *Space-Time and Beyond* (New York: Dutton, 1975).

3 See the popular discussion of these events in Zukav, *The Dancing Wu Li Masters* (London: Rider, 1979), pp. 308f.

4 *Ibid.*, pp. 317f.

5 David Bohm, 'Quantum Theory as an Indication of a New Order in Physics,' *Quantum Theory and Beyond*, ed. by Ted Bastin (New York: Cambridge University Press, 1971).

6 Lewis Thomas, *The Lives of a Cell* (New York: Bantam, 1975).

7 C.G. Jung, 'Synchronicity, An Acausal Connecting Principle,' *Collected Works*, vol. 8 (Princeton, New Jersey: Princeton

University Press, Bollingen Series XX, 1960).

8 Richard Wilhelm, *The I Ching or Book of Changes* (London: Routledge & Kegan Paul, 1973). Here he interprets the Tao as meaning.

9 The most notable attempt to connect physics, mathematics and analytical psychology is made by Marie-Louise von Franz in her *Number and Time* (Evanston, Illinois: Northwestern University Press, 1974). See also Arnold Mindell, 'Synchronizität,' in *Behandlungsmethoden in der Analytischen Psychologie*, ed. by U. Eschenbach, Fellbach-Oeffingen (Bonz Verlag, 1979). 'Synchronicity: An Investigation of the Unitary Background Patterning Synchronous Phenomena. (A Psychoid Approach to the Unconscious),' *Dissertation Abstracts International*, vol. 37, no. 2 (1976).

10 Arnold Mindell, *Dreambody* (Boston: Sigo Press, 1981; London: Routledge & Kegan Paul, 1984).

11 C.G. Jung, 'Review of the Complex Theory,' *Collected Works*, vol. 8.

12 *Dreambody*, op. cit., chapter 10.

13 J. Holten, 'The Roots of Complementarity,' *Eranos Jahrbuch*, 37 (1970), p. 50.

14 Werner Heisenberg, *Physics and Philosophy* (New York: Harper & Row, 1958), p. 41.

15 Zukav, *The Dancing Wu Li Masters*, op. cit., pp. 284ff.

16 In C.G. Jung's *Collected Works*, vol. 14, he expands upon the relationship of psychology to physics in terms of the 'Unus Mundus.' See, for example, para. 765ff.

17 C.G. Jung, *Collected Works*, vol. 8, para. 368ff.

18 Marie-Louise von Franz, *Number and Time*, op. cit., pp. 64-77.

19 David Finkelstein, 'Quantum Physics and Process Metaphysics,' *Physical Reality and Mathematical Description*, op. cit.

20 The discussion of this section was originally developed in my 'Synchronizität,' op. cit.

21 Don Juan, the shaman hero of Carlos Castaneda's *Journey to Ixtlan* (New York: Simon & Schuster, 1972), speaks in the first chapter of that book of events which match the mood and situation of a sorcerer who has adjusted himself to what we might call the Tao. These 'agreements form the world around us,' as he calls them are positive experiences which cluster about one's actions like variations on a musical theme.

22 David Finkelstein, 'Primitive Concept of Process,' (*Physical Reality and Mathematical Description*, op. cit.) formulates processes in physics as a new basis replacing time and space.

23 *Ibid.*

24 David Bohm, *Wholeness and the Implicate Order*, (London: Routledge & Kegan Paul, 1980), p. 11.

## CHAPTER 6 PROCESS MYTHOLOGY

1 Joseph Campbell, 'Man and Myth,' in *Voices and Visions* (New York: Harper & Row, 1976).
2 *Ibid.*
3 Marie-Louise von Franz, 'The Anti-Christ,' unpublished lecture.
4 *Ibid.*
5 Marie-Louise von Franz, *Time, Rhythm and Repose* (London: Thames & Hudson, 1978).
6 *Ibid.*
7 *Ibid.*
8 Arthur Avalon, *Serpent Power* (New York: Dover Publications, 1974).
9 Von Franz, *Time, Rhythm and Repose, op. cit.*
10 *Ibid.*
11 H. Ogawa, 'The Concept of Time in the Mithraic Mysteries,' *The Study of Time III*, ed. by J.T. Fraser, N. Lawrence and D. Park (New York: Springer Verlag, 1971).
12 Marie-Louise von Franz, 'Discussion and Comment,' in *The Study of Time III*, ed. by J.T. Fraser, N. Lawrence and D. Park (New York: Springer Verlag, 1971).
13 Isaac Asimov, *Energy and Life, An Exploration of the Physical and Chemical Basis of Modern Biology* (New York: Avon, 1972).
14 C.G. Jung, 'On Psychic Energy,' *Collected Works*, vol. 8 (Princeton, New Jersey: Princeton University Press, Bollingen Series XX, 1960).
15 Mircea Eliade, *Yoga: Immortality and Freedom* (Princeton, New Jersey: Princeton University Press, 1977), p. 272 (quote on dead men in life).
16 Von Franz, *Time Rhythm and Repose, op. cit.*, p. 8.
17 Werner Bohm, *Chakras, Lebenskrafte und Bewusstseinzentren im Menschen* (Weilheim Obb.: Otto Wilhelm Barth, 1966).

## CHAPTER 7 CHANNELS IN TAOISM

1 Raymond van Over, *Taoist Tales.*
2 Marcel Granet, *Das Chinesische Denken* (München: Piper Verlag, 1963), pp. 89, 246.
3 Helmut Wilhelm, *Eight Lectures on the I Ching* (New York: Harper Torchbooks, 1964), p. 18.
4 Lao Tsu, *The Tao Te Ching* (New York: Vintage Books, 1st Edition, 1972).
5 Shunryu Suzuki, *Zen Mind, Beginners Mind* (New York & Tokyo: Weatherhill, 1976).
6 Wilhelm, *The I Ching, Book of Changes, The Richard Wilhelm Translation*, rendered into English by Carl Baynes (London:

Routledge & Kegan Paul, 1973), p. 300.
7  See previous chapter.
8  *The I Ching, op. cit.*, p. 300.
9  *Ibid.*, p. 300.
10  C.G. Jung, 'Practical Use of Dream Analysis,' *Collected Works*, vol. 16 (Princeton, New Jersey: Princeton University Press, Bollingen Series XX, 1960).
11  C.G. Jung, 'Review of the Complex Theory,' *Collected Works*, vol. 8.
12  C.G. Jung, 'Psychological Aspects of a Mother Archetype,' *Collected Works*, vol. 9, para. 155.
13  Marie-Louise von Franz, *An Introduction to the Psychology of Fairy Tales* (Zürich, Switzerland: Spring Publications, 1973), pp. 9, 10. She puts it this way. 'In the unconscious all archetypes are contaminated with one another. It is as if several photographs were printed one over the other. They cannot be disentangled. This has probably to do with the relative timelessness and spacelessness of the unconscious. It is like a package of representations which are simultaneously present. Only when the conscious mind looks at it, is one motif selected. Thus for one scientist the mother is everything, for another everything is vegetation, and for another everything is solar myth. . .'
14  *The I Ching, op. cit.*, p. 264.
15  John Blofeld, *The I Ching, The Book of Changes* (New York: Dutton), pp. 61f. The introduction explains the use of incense and meditation in great detail.
16  *The I Ching, op. cit.*, p. L1
17  *Ibid.*, see Jung's introduction to the *I Ching*.

CHAPTER 8   PATTERNS IN THE *I CHING*

1  *The I Ching, The Book of Changes*, translated by John Blofeld (New York: Dutton, 1965).
2  *Ibid.*, pp. 266 and 269.
3  *Ibid.*, p. xxxvii.
4  *The I Ching, op. cit.*, pp. 359f.
5  *Ibid.*, p. 315.
6  Lao Tsu, *Tao Te Ching* (New York: Vintage Books, 1st Edition, 1972).
7  *Ibid.*, chapter 21.
8  R.G.H. Siu, *The Portable Dragon, The Western Man's Guide to the I Ching* (Cambridge, Mass.: M.I.T. Press, 1979), p. 405.

## CHAPTER 9   THE ALCHEMICAL OPUS

1   Lu K'uan Yu, *Taoist Yoga: Alchemy and Immortality* (London: Rider, 1972).
2   Mircea Eliade, *Yoga: Immortality and Freedom* (Princeton, New Jersey: Princeton University Press, 1972), pp. 274-92.
3   Marie-Louise von Franz, *Alchemical Active Imagination*, p. 1f. Here von Franz gives a brief, singularly clear introduction to the psychology and history of alchemy.
4   Stanislas Klossowski de Rola, *The Secret Art of Alchemy* (London: Thames & Hudson, 1973). Here a short version of alchemy is expressed with minimum interpretation.
5   C.G. Jung, 'Alchemical Studies,' *Collected Works*, vol. 13, and *Mysterium Coniunctionis, Collected Works*, vol. 14. (Princeton, New Jersey: Princeton University Press, Bollingen Series XX, 1960).
6   Klossowski de Rola, *op. cit.*
7   *Ibid.*
8   *Ibid.*
9   *Ibid.*
10   *Ibid.*
11   *Ibid.*
12   *Ibid.*
13   *Ibid.*
14   *Ibid.*
15   *Ibid.*, Klossowski quoting Don Pernety's *Dictionnaire Mytho-Hermetique.*
16   *Ibid.*
17   *Ibid.*
18   *Ibid.*
19   *Ibid.*
20   C.G. Jung, *Memories, Dreams and Reflection*, recorded and edited by Aniela Jaffe (New York: Vintage Books, Random House, 1965), p. 179.
21   Carlos Castaneda, *Journey to Ixtlan* (New York: Simon & Schuster, 1972).
22   John Blofeld, *The I Ching, The Book of Changes* (New York, N.Y.: Dutton and Co., Inc.), pp. 36, 37.
23   Klossowski de Rola, *op. cit.*
24   *Ibid.*
25   *Ibid.*
26   *Ibid.*
27   C.G. Jung, *Mysterium Coniunctionis, op. cit.*, p. 473.
28   *Ibid.*, para. 663f.
29   *Ibid.*
30   *Ibid.*
31   See Brad Steiger, *Medicine Power, The American Indian's Revival*

*of his Spiritual Heritage and Its Relevance for Modern Man* (New York: Doubleday, 1974); C.G. Jung, *Mysterium Coniunctionis, op. cit.*, para. 604.

# BIBLIOGRAPHY

Asimov, Isaac, *Energy and Life, An Exploration of the Physical and Chemical Basis of Modern Biology*, New York: Avon, 1972.

Avalon, Arthur, *The Serpent Power*, New York: Dover Publications, 1974.

Bandler, Richard and Grinder, John, *Frogs into Princes, Neuro-Linguistic Programming*, Moab, Utah: Real People Press, 1979.

——, *The Structure of Magic, A Book About Language and Therapy*, Palo Alto, Cal.: Science and Behavior Books, 1975.

Bateson, G., *Steps to an Ecology of Mind*, New York: Ballantine, 1972.

Berne, Eric, *Beyond Games and Scripts*, New York: Grove Press, 1977.

Blofeld, John, *The I Ching, The Book of Changes*, New York: Dutton, 1968.

Bohm, David, 'Quantum Theory As An Indication of a New Order in Physics,' in: *Quantum Theory and Beyond*, New York: Cambridge University Press, 1971.

——, *Wholeness and the Implicate Order*, London: Routledge & Kegan Paul, 1980.

Bohm, Werner, *Chakras, Lebenskrafte und Bewusstseinzentren im Menschen*, Weilhelm Obb.: Otto Wilhelm Barth, 1966.

Bry, Adelaide, *A Primer of Behavioral Psychology*, New York: New American Library, 1975.

Campbell, Joseph, 'Man and Myth,' in: *Voices and Visions*, New York: Harper & Row, 1976.

Capra, Fritjof, *The Tao of Physics*, Boulder, Col.: Shambhala, 1976.

Castaneda, Carlos, *Journey to Ixtlan*, New York: Simon & Schuster, 1972.

*The Concise Oxford Dictionary*, revised by E. McIntosh, London: Oxford University, 1964.

Dossey, Larry, *Space, Time and Medicine*, Boulder, Col: Shambhala, 1982.

Downing, George, *The Massage Book*, New York: Random House, 1972.

Dusen, Wilson van, 'The Phenomenology of a Schizophrenic Existence,' in: *Gestalt Is*, New York: Bantam Books, 1977.

Dychtwald, Ken, *Bodymind*, New York: Jove, 1978.

Ebin, Victoria, *The Body Decorated*, London: Thames & Hudson, 1979.

Einstein, Albert and Infeld, L., *The Evolution of Physics*, Cambridge: Cambridge University Press, 1971.

Eliade, Mircea, *Shamanism: Archaic Techniques of Ecstasy*, London: Routledge & Kegan Paul, 1970.

——, *Yoga: Immortality and Freedom*, Princeton, N.J.: Princeton University Press, 1977.

Ellis, Albert, *Humanistic Psychotherapy*, New York: McGraw-Hill, 1974.

Fabredga, H. and Manning, P.K., 'An Integrated Theory of Disease: Ladino-Mestizo Views of Disease in the Chiapas Highlands,' in: *Rediscovery of the Body*, New York: Dell, 1977.

Feldenkrais, Moshe, *Body and Mature Behavior*, New York: International Universities Press, 1973.

Feynman, R.P., 'The Theory of Positrons,' in: *Physical Review*, vol. 76, no. 6 (1949).

Finkelstein, David, 'Quantum Physics and Process Metaphysics,' in: *Physical Reality and Mathematical Description*, Holland: E. Reidel, 1974.

——, 'Primitive Concept of Process,' in: *Physical Reality and Mathematical Description*, Holland: E. Reidel, 1974.

Franz, Marie-Louis von, *Number and Time*, Evanston, Ill.: Northwestern University Press, 1974.

——, *Projection and Reflection in Jungian Psychology*, La Salle, Ill.: Open Court, 1980.

——, *Time, Rhythm and Repose*, London: Thames & Hudson, 1978.

——, 'The Anti-Christ,' unpublished lecture.

——, *Alchemical Active Imagination*, Dallas, Texas: Spring Publications, 1979.

——, *Patterns of Creativity Mirrored in Creation Myths*, Zürich, Switzerland: Spring Publications, 1972.

——, *Introduction to the Psychology of Fairy Tales*, Zürich, Switzerland: Spring Publications, 1973.

Franz, Marie-Louise von and Hillman, James, *Lectures on Jung's Typology*, New York: Spring Publications, 1971.

Granet, Marcel, *Das Chinesische Denken*, Münich, Germany: Piper-Verlag, 1963.

Grinder, John, see Bandler, Richard.

Hannah, Barbara, *Active Imagination*, Los Angeles: Sigo Press, 1981.

Heisenberg, Werner, *Physics and Philosophy*, New York: Harper & Row, 1958.

Herink, R., see *The Psychotherapy Handbook*.

Hillman, James and Franz, Marie-Louise von, *Lectures on Jung's*

*Typology*, New York: Spring Publications, 1971.

Holten, J., 'The Roots of Complementarity,' in: *Eranos Jahrbuch*, vol. 37 (1970).

Infeld, L., see Einstein, Albert.

Iyengar, B.K.S., *Light on Yoga, Yoga Dipika*, New York: Schocken Books, 1979.

Judge, A.S.N., *Development Through Alternation*, Brussels: Union of Interiation Associations, 1982.

Jung, C.G. (with M.L. von Franz, Joseph L. Henderson, Jolande Jacobi, Aniela Jaffe), *Man and His Symbols*, New York: Doubleday, 1965.

*The Collected Works of C.G. Jung*. Edited by Sir Herbert Read, Michael Fordham and Gerhard Adler. Translated by R.F.C. Hull (except for vol. 2). Princeton, New Jersey: Princeton University Press, (Bollingen Series XX) and London: Routledge & Kegan Paul, 1953-    . Cited throughout as *CW*. Volumes cited in this publication:

Vol. 6, *Psychological Types*, 1971.

Vol. 8, *The Structure and Dynamics of the Psyche*, 1960.

Vol. 11, *Psychology and Religion*, 1958.

Vol. 13, *Alchemical Studies*, 1967.

Vol. 14, *Mysterium Coniunctionis: An Inquiry into the Separation and Synthesis of Psychic Opposites in Alchemy*. 2nd Edition, 1970.

Vol. 16, *The Practice of Psychotherapy*, 1954.

Individual writings, with relevant volume of the *Collected Works* (see above):

'A Review of the Complex Theory,' *CW* 8, paras. 194-219.

'Synchronicity: An Acausal Connecting Principle,' *CW* 8, paras. 816-968.

'On Psychic Energy,' *CW* 8.

'The Transference,' *CW* 16, paras. 353-539.

*Memories, Dreams and Reflections*. New York, N.Y.: Vintage Books, Random House, 1965.

Klossowski, Stanislas de Rola, *The Secret Art of Alchemy*, London: Thames & Hudson, 1973.

Laszlo, Legeza, *Tao Magic*. London: Thames & Hudson, 1975.

———, *Tao: The Chinese Philosophy of Time and Change*, London: Thames & Hudson, 1973.

Lieban, Richard W., 'Medical Anthropology,' in: *Handbook of Social and Cultural Anthropology*, Chicago, Ill.: Rand McNally, 1973.

Lockhart, Russell A., 'Cancer in Myth and Dream,' *Spring*, 1977.

Lowen, Alexander, *Bioenergetics*, New York: Coward, McCann & Geoghegan, 1975.

———, *The Betrayal of the Body*, New York: Collier Books, 1973.

Manning, P.K., see Fabredaga, H.

Meier, C.A., 'A Jungian Approach to Psychosomatic Medicine,' in: *Journal of Analytical Psychology, vol. 8, no. 2* (1963).

Mindell, Arnold, *Dreambody*, Boston: Sigo Press, 1981; London: Routledge & Kegan Paul, 1984.
——, 'Der Korper in der Analytischen Psychologie,' in: *Behandlungsmethoden in der Jungscher Psychologies*, Fallbach-Oeffingen: Bonz Verlag, 1979.
——, 'Somatic Consciousness,' in: *Quadrant*, Jung Foundation, 1981.
——, 'Synchronicity: An Investigation of the Unitary Background Patterning Synchronous Phenomena. (A Psychoid Approach to the Unconscious),' *Dissertation Abstracts International*, vol. 37, no. 2 (1976).
——, 'Synchronizität,' in: *Behandlungsmethoden in der Analytischen Psychologie*, Fellbach-Oeffingen: Bonz Verlag, 1979.
——, *Working with the Dreaming Body*, London: Routledge & Kegan Paul, 1985.
Moreno, J.L., *Who Shall Survive?* New York: Beacon Press, 1952.
Morris, Desmond, *The Human Zoo*, New York: Dell, 1976.
Mumford, John, *Psychosomatic Yoga*, Wellingborough: Aquarian Press, 1976.
Muktananda, Swami Baba, *The Play of Consciousness*, California: Shree Gurudev Siddha Yoga Ashram, 1974.
Neuman, John von, *The Mathematical Foundations of Quantum Mechanics*, Princeton, N.J.: Princeton University Press, 1955.
Neidhart, John, *Black Elk Speaks: Being the Life Story of a Holy Man of the Ogalala Sioux*, Nebraska: University of Nebraska Press, 1961.
Ogawa, H., 'The Concept of Time in the Mithraic Mysteries,' in: *The Study of Time III*, New York: Springer Verlag, 1971.
Ogden, Thomas H., *Projective Identification*, New York: Jasan Aronson, 1982.
Over, Raymond van, ed. *Taoist Tales*, New York: The New American Library, 1973.
Oxford, *The Concise Oxford Dictionary*, 6th edn London: Oxford University Press, 1976.
Perls, Fritz, *Gestalt Therapy Verbatim*, Lafayette: Real People Press, 1969.
Philips, A.I. and Smith, G.W., *Couple Therapy*, New York: Collier Books, 1973.
*The Psychotherapy Handbook*, ed. Richie Herink, New York: Meridian, 1980.
Rawson, Philip, *Tantra: The Indian Cult of Ecstasy*, London: Thames & Hudson, 1973.
——. and Laszlo, L., *Tao Magic*, London: Thames & Hudson, 1975.
——. and Laszlo, L., *Tao: The Chinese Philosophy of Time and Change*, London: Thames & Hudson, 1973.
Reich, Wilhelm, *Character Analysis*, New York: Farrar, Straus & Giroux, 1968.

Rolf, Ida, 'Structural Integration,' in: *Confinaia Psychiatrica*, vol. 16 (1973).

Satir, Virginia, *Helping Families to Change*, Hays, Kansas: The High Plains Comprehensive Community Mental Center, 1972.

Shunryu, Suzuki, *Zen Mind, Beginner's Mind*, New York and Tokyo: Weatherhill, 1976.

Simonton, Carl I. and Simonton, Stephanie, 'Belief Systems and Management of the Emotional Aspects of Malignancy,' in: *Journal of Transpersonal Psychology*, vol. 7 (1975).

Simonton, Stephanie, see Simonton, Carl I.

Siu, R.G.H., *The Portable Dragon, The Western Man's Guide to the I Ching*, Cambridge, Mass.: M.I.T. Press, 1979.

Smith, G.W., see Phillips, A.I.

Spino, Michael, *Beyond Jogging, The Inner Spaces of Running*, New York: Berkeley, 1976.

Stapp, H., 'Theory of Reality,' in: *Foundations of Physics*, vol. 7 (1977).

Steiger, Brad, *Medicine Power, The American Indian's Revival of His Spiritual Heritage and Its Relevance for Modern Man*, New York: Doubleday, 1974.

Steiner, Claude M., *Scripts People Live By, Transactional Analysis of Life Scripts*, New York: Bantam, 1975.

Tansley, David, *Subtle Body, Essence and Shadow*, London: Thames & Hudson, 1977.

Thera, Nyanaponika, *The Heart of Buddhist Meditation*, New York: Weiser, 1962.

Thomas, Lewis, *The Lives of a Cell, Notes of a Biology Watcher*, New York: Bantam, 1979.

Toben, Bob, *Space-Time and Beyond*, New York: Dutton, 1975.

Tsu, Lao, *The Tao Te Ching*, New York: Vintage, 1972.

Watts, Alan, *The Book*, New York: Collier Books, 1968.

Webber, Andrew Lloyd and Rice, Tim, *Jesus Christ Superstar, A Rock Opera*, Decca Records: New York: 1970.

Weizacker, K.F., *Physical Reality and Mathematical Description*, Holland: E. Reidel, 1974.

Weith, Ilsa (translator), *The Yellow Emperor's Classic of Internal Medicine*, Berkeley, Cal.: University of California Press, 1966.

Wilhelm, Helmut, *Change: Eight Lectures on the I Ching*, New York: Harper Torchbooks, 1964.

Wilhelm, Richard, *The I Ching or Book of Changes*, London: Routledge & Kegan Paul, 1973.

Yablonsky, Lewis, *Psychodrama*, New York: Basic Books, 1976.

Yu, Lu K'uan, *Taoist Yoga: Alchemy and Immortality*, London: Rider, 1972.

Zukav, Gary, *The Dancing Wu Li Masters*, London: Rider, 1979.

# INDEX

126; amplification of, 16, 17, 25; binary, 103; and causality, 45, 56; composite, 19, 20; differentiation of, 15, 28; as dreamed-up reactions, 48-9, 50, 51; eye, 16, 17, 136; extraverted, 18-21; flickering of, 104-6, 107; incomplete, 35; of inflation, 42, 43; introverted, 18, 21, 33, 34; mixed, 18, 19; non-verbal, 39; picking up, 31, 141, 142; post-Einsteinian, 58, 63, 68; repression of, 54; and secondary process, 98, 111; superluminal, 59, 60; working with, 39 (see also Double signals)
Singing, 32-3
Skin, 96
Sleep: difficulties, 34
Smell, 15
Snake (see Serpent)
Social pressure, 138, 139
Social work, 53
Sol, 81
Solar principle, 129-30
Sound, 18, 19; waves, 42
Space, 61, 63, 65, 66, 67, 73, 85, 86, 94, 102
Speed of light, 42, 56, 59
Spirit, 135; in alchemy, 121; in *I Ching*, 97, 98, 108
Staffs, 81, 83, 95
Stars, 134
State-oriented: psychology, 12, 86, 93, 131; reality, 137
States, 11-2, 14, 74, 75-6, 86, 88; and dream universe, 63, 65, 66; in *I Ching*, 110; in sexuality, 52; in Taoism, 93-4
Static concepts, 93, 94
Stimulus-response theory, 9
Stomach: ache, 17, 25, 27, 28, 141; pain, 96, 103; troubles, 98; tumor, 105
'Stone of the philosophers', 121
'Stopping the world', 88-9
Story telling, 32-3
Strangling, 107
Stress, 86, 132
Stretching, 8
Stuttering, 31
Subtle body, 52, 81, 119

Sulphur, 129
Superluminal: communication, 58, 59; nature, 68; signals, 59, 60
Surgeon, 5
Symbols: Aion, 81-4; of Aquarian waterbearer, 74; bird, 76, 135; and body experiences, 34, 80; caelum, 138; devil, 35; dog, 37; egg, 126-7; of energy, 71, 80, 83, 84; gold, 119, 140; king, 137; kundalini, 80; lion, 81, 83, 95; Oceanos, 75-9; *prima materia*, 119; of process, 75-89, 137; queen, 137; salamander, 91; serpent, 75-6, 77, 79, 81, 83, 91, 95; staffs, 81, 83, 95; stars, 134; of time, 71, 75, 76, 77, 83; of ying-yang, 92, 93; of zodiac, 86
Symptoms, 9, 12, 38, 61, 79, 88; acute, 53; in dreams, 27; getting rid of, 127, 140; liberation from, 114, 115; as meaningful, 36;
Synchronicity, 3, 24, 55, 57, 60, 65, 68, 97, 112, 134, 142; as archetypal manifestation, 63; and dreambody work, 58-9, 60, 61

Talmudic literature, 139
Tantra, 119
Tantric yoga, 52, 125
Tao, 14, 48, 57, 89, 90, 139; according to Lao-Tsu, 115; concept of, 90-7; definition of, 91, 93, 95; and groups, 113; as process, 90-8, 108, 123; teaching of, 115-16
Taoism, 3, 6, 57; channel concepts in, 90-108, 110; and edges, 115; evolution of, 93-4; limitations of, 142; and process concepts, 71, 72, 90-108; static concepts of, 84, 93
Taoists, 67, 92, 110, 117, 123, 127, 140, 142; Chinese, 119; as process worker, 91-2, 93
*Tao Te Ching*, 6, 90, 91, 93, 115
Taste, 15
Telekinesis, 56
Telepathy, 55, 56, 57, 68
Tempo, 17, 19, 26
Tension, 80, 137, 140
Tezcatlipocas, 87, 95, 101
Theologian, 8

occupied, 24, 139; unoccupied, 24
'World soul', 81
Wu Tzu, 115-16

Xenophobia, 89

Yahweh, 72, 94
'Yang', 92, 93, 96, 100, 102, 103, 104
Yawning, 8
'Yin', 92, 93, 96, 100, 102, 103, 104

Yoga, 8, 80, 132; hatha, 52, 119;
 tantric, 52
Yogic powers, 140
Yogis, 52, 80, 85, 140

Zen: master, 115; tale, 115-16; texts,
 131
Zeus, 81
Zodiac, 75, 81, 86; and channels,
 85-6